WHY PERSONALIZATION WINS THE
CUSTOMER EXPERIENCE

�֯ ✤ �֯ ✳

MARKETING
IN THE
AI ERA

YANIV NAVOT
LIZ STEELMAN
SHANA PILEWSKI

HarperCollins
Leadership

An Imprint of HarperCollins

This book is written as a source of information only. The information contained in this book should by no means be considered a substitute for the advice, decisions, or judgment of the reader's professional or financial advisors. All efforts have been made to ensure the accuracy of the information contained in this book as of the date published. The author and the publisher expressly disclaim responsibility for any adverse effects arising from the use or application of the information contained herein.

Design by Neuwirth & Associates, Inc.

ISBN 978-1-4002-5354-8 (eBook)
ISBN 978-1-4002535-3-1 (HC)
ISBN 978-1-4041-2097-6 (custom)

Library of Congress Cataloging-in-Publication Data
Library of Congress Cataloging-in-Publication application has been submitted.

Printed in the United States of America

25 26 27 28 29 LBC 5 4 3 2 1

CONTENTS

FOREWORD

In a world that is changing at unprecedented speeds, the marketing landscape stands at the brink of a profoundly new paradigm. The convergence of a massive influx of data, tremendous cultural shifts, and dozens of emerging technologies from AI to AR are upending traditional marketing.

Put simply, classical marketing theories and concepts no longer work.

We have to reinvent, reimagine, and drastically change our approach to marketing. I call this new approach "quantum marketing." As brands navigate this new and dynamic marketing landscape, they are confronted with a crucial realization: The days of bombarding consumers with generic, promotional messages are over.

In a world saturated with information, meaningful experiences reign supreme. Brands must, therefore, seize every touchpoint, whether physical, digital, or a hybrid of both—engaging with consumers in new and exciting ways.

Vital to achieving this is the practice of personalization, through which brands can forge genuine connections that resonate with the individuality of each consumer. This is all possible in a new paradigm of technology, data, and consumer appetite! Armed with real-time insights, right-timed interactions, and hyperpersonalized consumer engagement, personalization is set to catapult to astonishing levels of impact.

The smartest brand strategies will center on creating authentic, tailored digital activations that complement one another. This will require marketers to invest, test, and learn to identify what works for their brands and, importantly, their consumers.

This book offers an excellent resource on this journey. It provides practical advice, strategies, and playbooks for embracing personalization in this new era of marketing.

Truly, the possibilities are as limitless as imagination itself.

—RAJA RAJAMANNAR,
Chief Marketing Officer of Mastercard

INTRODUCTION

The Key to a More Human Digital Experience

Picture a moment after AOL entered your home but before a thousand songs could fit in your pocket. You're sitting in a computer room—or at your office or at school—and searching the internet for the first time. Your initial instinct is to type a question into the search box. The results appear; but it's not anything you want. You try again, this time recalling a tip about Boolean logic. You translate your thoughts into searchable keywords, and suddenly, there it is: a page with the information you sought.

For some of you, this isn't a hypothetical scenario but a real memory of a time before search engine optimization. Before the era of googling everything, the human instinct was to communicate with computers as one would a bank teller, customer service agent, bookseller, or friend—on a personal level. The urge to use natural language was so strong that one company created an immensely popular search engine to accommodate it. But technology wasn't advanced enough, and the internet, built on code that limited inputs to yes or no, forced humans to adjust.

As the internet left the confines of computer rooms and found its way into our pockets, humanity adapted. We learned to communicate with machines more efficiently, stripping queries and inputs of any nuanced meaning, boiling them down to basic data points that carried their own context.

Over the next decade and beyond, digital interactions became the norm. Digital natives like millennials and Gen Zers learned to "like" and "subscribe" their way to the information they sought, along the way creating online "identities" that fit into market segments. And as baby boomers and Gen Xers began to embrace technology in their daily lives, tech companies found they had to make the digital experiences more "user-friendly." Rather than presenting legible identities to machines like their younger peers, they left subtle clues about who they were and what they preferred with every click, scroll, and purchase.

With more people online than ever before, companies collected this data at an unprecedented level. There was soon too much to handle, so the companies invented algorithms to sort through it all, dictating "if this, then that." Still the algorithms weren't good enough to sort through all the incoming data. We needed a more proactive approach. A/B testing entered the scene, letting visitors vote with their clicks, with the majority of clicks being deemed the winner. We shifted the way we live to accommodate not only the collection of data, but how we could measure, iterate, and optimize it endlessly. Offline, the culture was ruled by the 51 percent too. Pop stars and superheroes rose to the top of the charts and stayed there, amassing billions of dollars rather than millions.

While the KPIs were stellar, maybe this "winner takes all" mentality was doing more harm than good. Different people have different needs and come from different contexts and bring with them different expectations. Yes, some people are willing to trust a brand's standard issue experience, but others want an experience more relevant and tailored to them. Could we create an internet where we serve different experiences to different people?

My journey began about here, with the concept of what we now know as personalization. When I joined Dynamic Yield a decade ago, we focused on helping online publishers and retailers use data on individual user behavior to create cohesive experiences from the moment the person clicked on an ad. Using targeting and basic rules, we developed algorithms that dynamically allocated traffic in real time, like multiarmed bandits. Quickly we realized that even testing shouldn't be a blanket rule.

Over the next decade, we worked with advancing AI and machine learning capabilities that make it possible to process humanity's yes and no inputs into a broader picture. Deep learning models excel at handling vast and complex data. While we're still limited to "if this, then that" thinking, we can now detect intricate patterns, associations between data points, and continuously refine predictions in seconds. These advances have led to always-on "recommender systems" that enable brands to create hyperpersonalized experiences for all users, even on their first site visit. For example, without knowing any purchase history or explicit preferences for a new user, a retailer can still offer highly relevant recommendations by analyzing data from similar users—browsing patterns, purchase history, time spent on specific product pages. A deep learning model might detect that first-time visitors who view outdoor gear often explore sustainable products. This knowledge then allows the retailer to instantly curate a selection of eco-friendly items for this new shopper who's interested in hiking equipment.

This example is industry specific and limited to a real customer use case. But AI's potential applications at the intersection of customer experience and marketing are vast, and they bring us closer to our innate vision of what technology could be. Services like Netflix, Spotify, and Amazon are proof: They've led the way in offering personalization and reshaped customer expectations entirely. People don't want the one-size-fits-all internet anymore; they want a more human experience that recognizes more context. And that goes for all companies, whether it's an airline, bank, or retailer. They want experiences that speak to the individuality of Gen Zers and millennials and the seamless, frictionless interactions that baby boomers and Gen X customers expect. And they're willing to pay a premium for this too.

After more than a decade of envisioning a more human-centered internet but living with a one-size-fits-all experience, I am confident that AI-powered personalization can find that clear human signal amid the noise of data and add real empathy and emotion into the internet. We're on the brink of achieving a digital world that's as unique as each individual using it, but businesses need to learn how to transcend the noise, understand their customers' wants and needs on an emotional level, and deliver a clear, personalized signal to each individual. Marketers who master this will reap transformative rewards. Those who delay their journey will not only lose their competitive edge but will also risk falling further behind. Think of this book as your guide, offering practical advice and real-world examples to help you unlock the power of personalization and navigate your way to a personalized future.

Whether you're just starting out or looking to refine your marketing approach, these pages provide the knowledge and inspiration you need to connect with your audience on a deeper level and build the emotional bonds that foster lasting brand loyalty.

—YANIV NAVOT,
Chief Marketing Officer of Dynamic Yield by Mastercard

PART ONE

SETTING OFF ON YOUR PERSONALIZATION JOURNEY: AN OVERVIEW

Welcome to the first step on your personalization journey. Providing personalized experiences has become essential for businesses in all sectors: It's no longer just an added value but a critical factor. Customers now expect tailored experiences from brands and will give these preferred brands repeat business and ongoing engagement. While investing in personalization technology may seem like a silver bullet, the hard part comes after onboarding, as we will explore in this book. To succeed in this new paradigm of marketing, organizations need a winning combination of technology, expertise, processes, and methodologies to achieve desired results. As you read this book, it'll be clear that the journey to pioneering personalization is a marathon, not a sprint.

This book is a practical guide for mastering personalization in this new world. Whether you are new to personalization or a seasoned pioneer, this book will teach you how to create a personalization "center of excellence" that encompasses the optimal processes, teams, and methodologies. Our objective is to help you plan and create a sustainable program that not only adapts to current demands but also generates revenue impact for the future. By the end of this book, you'll understand what it takes to turn your personalization program from a project into a marketing powerhouse.

This first part will help you understand the basics of personalization. If you're familiar with personalization, move on to part 2. But it might be helpful to review some of the specific terminology. For example, if you use personalization strategies daily, you may understand many concepts but not be able to refer to them by name. Articulating these ideas, like the difference between an "unknown unknown" and a "known unknown" customer, might unlock a new segmentation strategy for your company.

TRANSMISSION FROM YOUR FUTURE

As you learn, we'll send you "Transmissions" like these—messages packed with important details, tips, and tricks that will be most helpful when you're out there putting your knowledge to the test, like picking a personalization engine, onboarding your CRM data, and setting up your Evergreen Personalization Zones.

Before we put personalization into practice, we'll dive deeper into why personalization is an essential marketing strategy for businesses today. To set your organization up for success, you'll need to understand the immediate results of investing in personalization, how it can set you up for long-term success, and even why shirking investment could ruin your brand's future. Since embedding personalization into an organization's culture is imperative for its success, this part will also prepare you to teach about personalization's potential at every level, cultivate a deep, cross-functional culture of experimentation, and evolve previous practices and mindsets. Beyond the technology, we'll also discuss which critical functions you'll need to start and scale a personalization team across business units.

Then, we'll develop your personalization strategy from the ground up. From here, we'll dive into a scalable process plus show you different methodologies you can adopt. After you feel confidently prepared to grow your program, we'll look ahead at what personalization might hold in the future.

We think it's vital to see real-life examples of personalization in practice, so the final portion of this book is a playbook packed with proven strategies and real-world examples from hundreds of successful campaigns. Spanning industries and channels, these examples will help you see what is possible with personalization today and inspire you to create your marketing strategies for tomorrow.

GET STRAIGHT TO THE SIGNAL

We know attention spans are shorter than ever, so each section ends with the highlights needed to get you on your way.

Before we go ahead, let's get back to the basics.

Chapter One

THE BASICS

✖ ✛ ✖ ✳

WHAT IS PERSONALIZATION?

Imagine a world where every interaction with a brand feels like it was crafted just for you. Where websites anticipate your needs, apps deliver recommendations you'll love, and marketing messages resonate with your deepest desires. This is personalization's promise, and it's transforming the way businesses understand and form long-lasting connections with their customers.

Personalization provides the most relevant experience to a particular audience or individual. Personalization is made possible with personalization engines, which help brands automate the collection and interpretation of customer insights and determine, deliver, and measure the optimum experience for an individual customer or prospect based on their past interactions, current context, and predicted intent.

TRANSMISSION FROM YOUR FUTURE:
THE TOOLS OF THE TRADE

When embarking on a personalization journey, it's crucial to understand the capabilities that make a personalization engine effective. Key features to look for include:

A unified dataset: The ability to collect and harmonize data from diverse sources is fundamental. This ensures a comprehensive understanding of customer interactions across various channels, such as web, app, and in-store. A unified dataset enables the creation of detailed audience segments, offers insights into audience behaviors, and highlights opportunities for targeted engagement.

Open architecture: An engine with an open architecture is essential for seamless integration with existing marketing technologies. This flexibility minimizes the need for extensive engineering work, speeds up the deployment process, and potentially lowers the overall costs associated with your marketing technology stack.

Decisioning and activation logic: Look for a system that employs advanced analytics and machine learning to automate decision-making. This includes managing and optimizing a growing number of targeted experiences across various digital platforms, regions, and currencies. Effective decisioning and activation logic supports running intricate tests, setting up variations, triggering messages, and building segments, thereby enhancing operational efficiency, scalability, and ensuring personalized experiences for each customer.

It's important to remember, however, that setting the foundation for personalization can take time; it's a journey. Brands don't need to have everything in place from the start, so long as they partner with a solution that can work with what they have today and that will allow them to gradually expand their technology stack.

PERSONALIZATION CHANNELS AND TOUCHPOINTS

Effective personalization varies across different marketing channels and touchpoints. It tailors content, products, offers, and complete customer experiences on websites, in emails, through native mobile apps, and even in physical retail environments such as in-store kiosks, drive-thrus, and more. Each channel offers unique opportunities for personalization, with the end goal of delivering a unified customer experience.

Websites

Website personalization comes in many different shapes and sizes. It encompasses a variety of techniques and use cases, each tailored to achieve specific goals for different customer segments or scenarios. From targeted content or product recommendations to dynamic web page layouts, individualized banners, and personalized messages, marketers can meticulously test, refine, and tailor these experiences to create a "just for you"–type experience for every visitor.

And with more than 60 percent of web traffic originating from mobile devices, personalization for mobile websites becomes essential. Our phones might reveal more about us than we think. Studies show differences between iPhone and Android customers, especially in online shopping habits. iPhone customers spend more than Android customers overall, across various markets and product categories.

Extending personalization from desktop to mobile websites allows brands to dynamically adapt content, notifications, layouts, and recommendations based on individual preference, purchase history, and data like browsing behavior, device type, and location to create a seamless and engaging mobile experience for each customer.

Emails

Email remains a marketing powerhouse for many brands because it delivers high ROI and direct customer connection. Thanks to interactive elements, personalization, and automation, marketers can send more engaging and effective emails. Email personalization delivers tailored content and campaigns according to subscribers' unique identifiers, such as location, loyalty status, shopping behavior, and affinities.

Allowing connections to be built beyond their website, brands can use personalized email strategies to capture their customer's attention at every critical moment, whether helping them pick up where they left off, delivering relevant content and recommendations, guiding them to learn more about the company, or offering exclusive benefits.

Native Mobile Apps

Mobile app personalization expands upon the benefits of mobile personalization, offering the competitive benefit of requiring customers to sign in to use the app. Because of this, mobile apps offer brands boundless opportunities for zero-party and first-party data capture to provide additional context and build rich customer profiles that can be deployed across platforms. This owned-and-operated channel additionally can deepen customer engagement and loyalty with in-app messages, push notifications, and triggered emails.

Physical Retail Environments

In-store personalization includes digital kiosks (including drive-thrus), personalized in-store offers, point-of-sale, and interactive experiences. Personalization in these settings can be based on past orders, time of day, and weather conditions to suggest relevant items.

Triggered Messages

Sending the right messaging at the right time can positively impact conversion rates. You can nudge customers to complete actions depending on their behavior and couple it with product recommendations, educational content, or offers in personalized emails, push notifications, or SMS to help close the conversion loop.

Omnichannel Experiences

Today's consumers interact with a company across channels, perhaps browsing a site once, then clicking on an email and later scrolling through a mobile app. These interactions should feel cohesive, and consumers expect companies to tailor these experiences, no matter the channel. Marketers can create omnichannel campaigns by delivering personalized experiences for each consumer throughout their journey, ensuring consistent and cohesive engagement.

Now that we've explored the channels of personalization, let's go over the structure of personalized marketing.

CAMPAIGNS, EXPERIENCES, AND VARIATIONS

Campaigns are the packages in which marketers deliver personalization to a customer. They are the components that display personalized content, offers, or products on a channel (or, in more complex cases, across channels). Experiences are what is delivered to the customer, and variations are the different versions of experiences that audience segments within each experience receive (we'll get more in-depth with this later).

Now that we've unlocked what personalization looks like on the front end, let's look behind the curtain and dive into what fuels the experiences in the background: data.

DATA: THE FUEL OF PERSONALIZATION

The key to personalization's possibilities, benefits, and current challenges boils down to understanding how personalization

Personalization campaign hierarchy

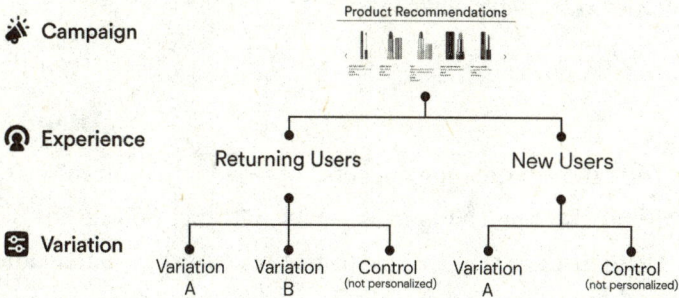

Think of campaigns as the "where," experiences as the "whom," and variations as the "what."

engines source, use, and build upon data—all of which we'll dive into for this section.

Simply, personalization solutions ingest and analyze data to determine what experiences and variations should be delivered.

TRANSMISSION FROM YOUR FUTURE:
THE 360-DEGREE MISCONCEPTION

Organizations commonly overestimate the amount and scope of data needed to personalize meaningfully. While the holy grail of personalization is a cohesive dataset that establishes a 360-degree or single view of the customer and will lead to more tailored options—you don't need this at the outset. A complete view of the customer is something an organization works toward

---

in its personalization journey. Too often, this misconception prevents brands from even starting.

You can reap the many benefits of personalization by looking at several different data sources—many of which you already have.

Explicit data refers to customer relationship management (CRM) data collected about a customer or so-called zero-party data, which a customer has explicitly provided through surveys and registration forms.

TRANSMISSION FROM YOUR FUTURE:
YOUR ORGANIZATION'S CRM IS A GOLD MINE

Onboarding your organization's CRM data into your personalization provider is an invaluable step toward this single view of the customer, as it enables you to match a CRM profile and an online visitor. You can onboard demographic data (gender, age, marital status, education, and so on), geographic data (billing and shipping country, city, and so on), interests and preferences, buyer persona, and internal segments captured by your business intelligence tools (VIP client, frequent buyer, and so on). This information is considered first-party data and lays a needed foundation for targeting your existing customers as efficiently and accurately as possible, making them feel at home as you tailor their experience and creating lasting emotional connections with your brand.

Behavioral (or implicit) data refers to the data collected from meaningful customer interactions such as clicks (pre- or postlogin), number of page views, URLs visited, or conversion events like application completion, signups, current page (such as a specific URL, the home page, a category page), and more.

Contextual data relates to surrounding circumstances and preferences that influence customer interactions, such as location (a customer's current country, region, or city), time of day, device type and details (desktop, mobile, tablet; operating system; browser), weather conditions, and so on.

Third-party data includes information collected and aggregated from outside sources, like a digital management platform (DMP) or customer relationship management platform (CRM), as valuable data sets to build segments.

TRANSMISSION FROM YOUR FUTURE:

BALANCING DATA ENRICHMENT AND GRANULARITY

IS CRITICAL

Combining data sources will allow you to get increasingly granular in your personalization: The more data you have about your potential buyer, the more the messaging can match their needs and interests. The more criteria applied, however, the greater the likelihood an individual may not meet the targeting conditions. Too many microsegments can result in personalization only affecting small pockets of traffic, minimizing the incremental revenue gain associated with these efforts.

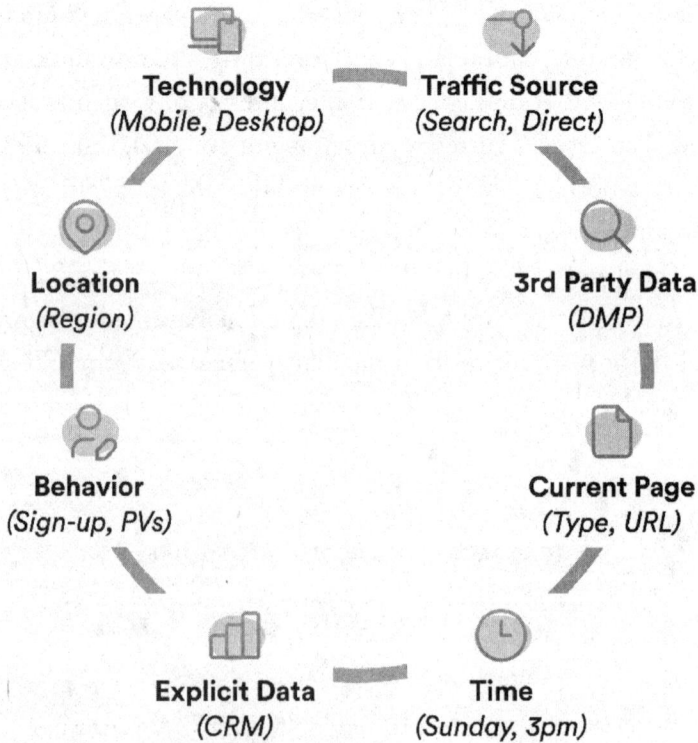

Technology
(Mobile, Desktop)

Traffic Source
(Search, Direct)

Location
(Region)

3rd Party Data
(DMP)

Behavior
(Sign-up, PVs)

Current Page
(Type, URL)

Explicit Data
(CRM)

Time
(Sunday, 3pm)

Types of data used for web personalization

ANONYMOUS VERSUS KNOWN CUSTOMERS

Personalization is relatively easy and accurate when you have rich customer data on "known" visitors—or those already in your database. For example, the customer fills out an individual questionnaire at onboarding, and all interactions after that consider this data. This, by the way, is why businesses in all industries have heavily invested in customer loyalty programs—and why brands like Amazon, Netflix, and Spotify encourage their customers to stay logged in, whether they are browsing on their phone or computer.

But you can also achieve personalization with a completely new—or unknown—customer. It's imperative to provide a tailored experience for this audience segment. The average website sees most of its traffic from anonymous visitors—that is, people who have never given you their email addresses. These could be first-time visitors to your site or returning visitors who are still not part of your CRM.

With such a large pool of visitors, businesses need to find ways to identify intent and preferences in real time as part of their personalization strategy and drive action with these customers. But while you might think that only a sliver of your audience is identifiable, it doesn't necessarily mean you can't get more personal with them.

In this bucket of "unknown customers" lies a group of people who can be considered "known unknowns"—people you don't know by name or email but can identify based on implicit and contextual data.

Through various techniques, brands can fill in the blanks in their anonymous visitor profiles and reduce the amount of genuinely unknown customers. Generally speaking, you can source this data from three areas:

- **Self-reported**, such as through web forms, online surveys, questionnaires, and so on (a strategy sometimes referred to as *self-segmentation* or *zero-party data collection*).
- **Digitally exhausted** based on browsing and purchasing behavior, scrolls, clicks, referral data, geolocation, and so on.
- **Profiled** through third-party data collaboration platforms that provide information collected from outside sources and aggregated by a DMP or customer data platform (CDP).

You can learn a lot about an unknown customer and their goal or purpose on your website by collecting, aggregating, and analyzing data from multiple sources. Anonymous visitors constantly leave clues as they interact with your digital channels. Serving them a static experience is a huge, missed opportunity as opposed to serving more relevant experiences. Organizations that learn to capitalize on this data can deliver digital customer experiences that meet individual needs and help customers find what they're looking for faster.

For example, when a visitor lands on a website, an organization can discern contextual data, such as their location or device type. In response, they can offer experiences with regional promotions (such as free shipping offers tailored by zip code), offers related to their local weather forecast (such as offering jackets and coats for visitors from cold-weather locations versus shorts and swimwear for warm-weather visitors), or messaging that addresses their device type (such as deals for iPhone holders).

Suppose a retailer looks to collect more data in exchange for deeper personalization. In that case, they can float a questionnaire campaign that asks the customer to provide explicit data (like their preferred brands, shoe styles, and so on) and, in return, deliver personalized recommendations tailored directly to their input. They might even ask the customer to save these results by providing an email address, helping transform this unknown customer into a known one.

But even if a customer doesn't interact with a targeted experience, a brand can still use customer behavioral data, such as their browsing history (what type of items they were looking at, the time they spent on a particular brand or page category, interactions with sales, or even reviews), and use this data to personalize.

As time passes, brands can collect more data, learning more about their anonymous customers via their browsing behavior, frequency of visits, and what interests them. These micro actions can be progressively used to profile different audience segments of anonymous customers, understanding their interests, preferences, and intent without personally identifiable information, and figuring out the best pathways to convert them to known customers. Over time, by connecting, matching, and syncing contextual data to anonymous customer IDs, that bucket of "unknown unknowns" becomes smaller and smaller.

A customer can be targeted according to any available data source, and there are many conditions brands can use simultaneously to ensure the right experience is delivered to the right user at the right time.

Broken out by high-level categories:

AUDIENCE CONDITIONS	DESCRIPTION
Location	The country, region, or city a customer is located in.
Technology	A customer's device type (desktop, mobile, tablet), operating system, browser, and even screen resolution.
Traffic sources	The specific traffic source of a visiting customer, be it direct or paid, via referral, search, or social.
Third-party data	Information about a customer that has been collected from outside sources and aggregated by a DMP.
Behavior	Important customer interactions such as clicks, add-to-carts, or purchase events, as well as the number of page views, URLs visited, and so on.
Explicit data	CRM data that has been collected about a customer or has been provided intentionally through surveys and registration forms.
Time	The select dates, days of the week, or time of day the experience is to be served to a customer.
Current page	The type of page a customer lands on, whether it's a specific URL, the home page, a product detail page (PDP), or the cart page.

Although third-party data represents the largest percent of site traffic containing this data, it is the least accurate to base your personalization on. Visitor tracking represents the next largest share (~60 percent), with a medium degree of accuracy—it is, however, effective for understanding overall traffic patterns and can be leveraged for bettering the anonymous visitor's time on site.

Both site behavior captured by algorithms and CRM data are considered the most accurate and, while small in size, should make for highly relevant interactions among returning and loyal visitors.

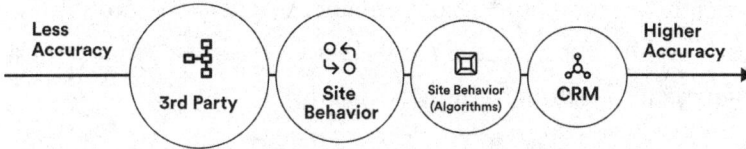

Size and accuracy of common data sources used for website personalization

A personalization program that combines different types of data sources will yield the best results.

DATA PROTECTION AND PRIVACY

In an evolving landscape of data protection, spearheaded by pivotal regulations like the General Data Protection Regulation (GDPR), the California Consumer Privacy Act (CCPA), and the ongoing phaseout of third-party cookies, brands are compelled to reassess their marketing strategies for collecting and utilizing personal data. These regulations necessitate obtaining explicit consent from individuals before tracking their online behavior, using cookies for experimentation, personalization, or attribution tracking. This transformation marks a significant paradigm shift in the definition, processing, utilization, and international transfer of personal information.

Understanding GDPR

The GDPR is a comprehensive framework for privacy and data protection. Its objective is to standardize privacy and data protection across the EU, ensuring the protection of residents' personal data. This regulation supersedes the EU's 1995 privacy directive, introducing new concepts and modifications to the existing privacy and data protection framework. These include stricter consent requirements, enhanced rights for data subjects, such as the right to access, rectify, delete, or port their data, and significant penalties for noncompliance.

Insights into CCPA

The CCPA represents a significant milestone in privacy rights and consumer protection for California residents. Effective from January 1, 2020, this statute grants Californians extensive rights concerning their personal information, including the right to know, delete, and opt out of the sale of their personal data, alongside protections against discrimination for exercising these rights. Applicable to any profit-driven entity that collects consumer personal data and conducts business in California, the CCPA sets benchmarks in privacy rights, influencing similar regulations in other jurisdictions.

TRANSMISSION FROM YOUR FUTURE:

THE IMPORTANCE OF GDPR AND ITS GLOBAL REACH

The GDPR's influence extends beyond the EU, applying to any organization that processes the personal data of EU residents, regardless of the organization's location. This global applicability ensures that virtually every significant website worldwide must comply with GDPR if it handles data from EU visitors. The regulation's broad scope underscores the importance of adhering to its provisions for organizations worldwide, including those in North America, Asia, and beyond.

The Role of Personalization Engines in GDPR Compliance

Personalization engines, acting as data processors, play a crucial role in helping data controllers manage customer data in compliance with GDPR. These engines provide the infrastructure and tools necessary for businesses to allow their customers to:

1. inquire about the data collected on them;
2. opt out of tracking; and
3. request the deletion of all previously stored data.

By facilitating these processes, personalization engines enable organizations to honor the rights of individuals under GDPR, thereby contributing to a more transparent and respectful handling of personal consumer data.

Delivering Responsible Personalization

Beyond the requirements posed by new legislation such as GDPR and CCPA, consumers themselves have become increasingly perceptive and protective of how their personal data is used. Privacy can no longer be viewed in a vacuum, and more companies are beginning to proactively assess their data strategies and the technologies that support them. It's so important to partner with vendors that operate with the highest set of privacy standards so that their practices are transparent, your data is protected, and the right controls are in place for how you go about using it. Only then can responsible personalization be achieved for the safe and compliant delivery of tailored customer experiences.

We've covered the basics of personalization. Let's explore how these foundational blocks add up to real value for your business—now and in the future.

GET STRAIGHT TO THE SIGNAL: PERSONALIZATION EXPLAINED

WHAT IS IT?

Personalization is tailoring experiences for specific audience groups or individual customers across various channels like websites, emails, and apps. It uses data to understand customer preferences and deliver relevant content, offers, and recommendations.

WHY IS IT IMPORTANT?

- It creates a more relevant and engaging experience for customers.
- It increases conversion rates and overall ROI.
- It builds stronger customer relationships and loyalty.

HOW DOES IT WORK?

Personalization engines analyze data from various source types, including:

- explicit data: customer information from forms and surveys;
- behavioral data: website interactions like clicks and page views; and
- contextual data: location, time of day, device type, and so on.

Based on this data, the engine delivers personalized experiences to each customer, such as:

- tailored content and product recommendations;
- personalized offers and promotions; and
- dynamic website layouts and messages.

CHALLENGES

- Data privacy regulations put guardrails on how data can be collected and used. Make sure you understand it well.
- Striking the balance between personalization and user privacy is needed and requires certain controls to be in place, which trusted vendors can help you navigate and set the technological foundation for.
- Unifying different data sources can be challenging at times but will help you deliver more relevant and cohesive experiences.

GETTING STARTED

- No need for a complete 360-degree view of the customer at the outset. Drop the myth, keep it real.
- Start with existing data sources like CRM and website analytics.
- Use self-segmentation tactics to collect explicit customer data in return for tailored experiences.

REMEMBER

- Personalization is a journey, not a destination.
- Continuously learn and improve your personalization strategy.

Chapter Two

THE BUSINESS

✕ ✦ ✖ ✳

THE BENEFITS OF PERSONALIZATION

Personalization is increasingly recognized as a cornerstone of a positive customer experience, offering a kaleidoscope of benefits for both consumers and brands alike. The evolution of personalization technology has significantly transformed consumer expectations, leading to a growing demand for customized experiences in every facet of daily life.

The impact of personalization in the realm of e-commerce is particularly striking. Research shows that nearly 90 percent of consumers are swayed by personalized online shopping experiences. Similarly, an almost equal percentage of marketers report a noticeable effect on revenue growth attributed to e-commerce personalization efforts. This strong connection between personalized experiences and commercial success underscores the critical need for businesses to invest in and continually improve their personalization strategies.

By focusing on personalization, companies can not only meet but exceed customer expectations, fostering loyalty and driving business growth in the process. The dynamic nature of consumer behavior necessitates an agile approach to personalization, one that can adapt to the ever-changing preferences and behaviors of the market.

On the brand side, personalization affects several key performance indicators (KPIs), driving:

Increased Acquisition ROI: By tailoring customer experiences based on initial interactions, brands can connect more effectively with their audience, creating an emotional bond that enhances the return on investment from marketing campaigns.

Enhanced Engagement: Companies can significantly boost customer engagement through personalized communications and offers. This approach keeps customers involved and interested throughout their journey with a brand.

Optimized Customer Behavior: Tailored messaging encourages customers to act in a way that aligns with a business's overall objectives, for example, using a new feature or engaging with a promotion.

Stronger Customer Loyalty: By understanding and catering to individual preferences and needs, brands can develop more meaningful relationships with their customers.

Long-Term Revenue Growth: Personalized experiences foster repeat business and long-term customer loyalty, which contribute to a sustainable increase in revenue.

WHY PERSONALIZATION IS IMPORTANT NOW

Over the past few years, personalization has evolved from a mere luxury to an indispensable tool as brands vie for consumer attention. In the digital jungle, amid the cacophony of noise and fierce competition, consumers gravitate toward brands that offer relevant, engaging, and convenient experiences across all channels. For customers, personalization unlocks the doors to enhanced discovery, strengthens emotional connections, and builds unwavering brand trust.

As brands leverage customer data to anticipate needs and proactively address them, the line between promoting products (marketing) and delivering exceptional service (customer experience) becomes increasingly thin. This convergence necessitates a customer-centric approach that prioritizes understanding individual preferences and delivering value with every interaction.

This paradigm shift not only bolsters brand retention and revenue potential but also caters efficiently to the ever-evolving desires of the modern consumer. Personalization has the power to deliver on the promise of a new era of customer focus, reshaping engagement dynamics.

THE OPPORTUNITY COST ASSOCIATED WITH FORGOING YOUR PERSONALIZATION PLANS

As customer expectations rise, businesses can't afford to maintain the status quo—they need to deliver the experiences of tomorrow rather than what people see as the current standard today. It's a hard reality. Customer loyalty isn't guaranteed. Even the most successful disruptors of our time struggle with staying on the cutting edge. It's why we're seeing giants like Netflix and Amazon not simply resting on their laurels but turning to strategies like personalization to meet their customers' unique needs.

Tech-savvy customers prioritizing relevance, ease, and enjoyment are ditching their once-favorite brands that no longer meet their needs, creating an entirely new battleground. Marketers are now expected to compete solely on the basis of their customer experience. With its ability to deliver on all three promises, personalization has subsequently increased in importance, ascending the throne as a top strategic priority within the larger business strategy.

Those who ignore the current world order do so at their peril, as poor personalization efforts can lead consumers to switch companies. Businesses shouldn't invest in a tailored customer journey because they can squeeze more from their current customers. They should invest in it because if they don't, they will have fewer customers tomorrow, which is why it's so imperative personalization plans get underway as soon as possible.

Given what we know about the future of personalization, the more time passes, the greater the cost of not having committed— the impact of which can have serious repercussions. Here are some areas where brands will end up paying, which will steadily compound over time.

Narrowing Economic Profit: Foregone profits result in unnecessary overhead and missed opportunities to innovate.

Increasing Competitor Intelligence: It's highly likely your competitors are already testing, tailoring, iterating, and improving experiences while you sit still.

Steepening Learning Curve: Lost time and learning lead to a more significant barrier to entry further down the road.

Rising Consumer Demands: Baseline expectations are only getting higher, making efforts to modernize more difficult.

While the cost of forgoing personalization can be detrimental to economic profit, businesses pay consequences far beyond revenue; the adverse effects trickle down to your marketing technology stack, data, team, and customers.

Fragmented Customer Experiences: Inconsistent experience during significant customer interactions may damage brand relations.

Deteriorating Data: Campaign messages become less and less relevant as consumer behavior evolves.

Outdated Marketing Technology Stack: Siloed systems trap data and create inefficiencies in implementation.

Stunting Organizational Success: Underwhelming performance hurts team morale and employee retention.

The personalization opportunity of today is already a requirement for tomorrow. This progression underlines the importance of integrating personalization into various aspects of business strategy. The dialogue around personalization should not only focus on its immediate benefits but also consider its role in shaping the future of business–customer relationships. By cultivating a culture of innovation and continuous learning, organizations can navigate the complexities of personalization, ensuring they remain relevant in a rapidly evolving digital landscape.

Start with a Sponsor

Over time, the conviction in the value of personalization typically grows within a company's leadership. But a significant barrier to its adoption often lies in whether you can secure the support of a committed executive sponsor.

Such a sponsor is pivotal in fostering a culture of personalization within the organization and advancing the company's strategic vision. Their role encompasses advocating internally, educating on the prerequisites for success, and facilitating collaboration among different stakeholders and departments. Without this leadership, personalization initiatives may falter, especially among team members who may not fully understand its relevance to the overarching business strategy or its personal implications for them.

Having a sponsor will foster acceptance and commitment, reducing friction from those more resistant to change—a problem many organizations face that can run the risk of stunting or even snuffing out new ideas and their blossoming programs.

One Sponsor, a Whole Team of Impact

A genuine commitment to succeeding with personalization requires the organization to align on the overall model—from defining and aligning on a vision to forecasting the financial return and then organizing teams to support the new processes.

With such a massive responsibility to a program, how do marketers help champion the right folks, communicate individual responsibilities, and update current operating methods to improve efficiencies? It starts by sharing the vision of personalization.

FRAMING THE VISION OF PERSONALIZATION

To get everyone on board, brands should first define a universally agreed-upon vision for personalization across the organization. Despite growing recognition for the practice of personalization, a few common objections can still distract from the benefits. Here's how to handle objections from other collaborators.

"It can wait." As you already know, the risk of revenue loss to competitors who have already embraced or are about to embrace personalized experiences increases as time goes on. Simultaneously, the cost of adhering to conventional methods also escalates.

The delay in adopting personalization puts businesses at a significant disadvantage. Customers, whose expectations continue to rise, will not pause for companies to upgrade their operations; they demand tailored and relevant services. Addressing these needs requires a relentless dedication to innovation, a journey with no endpoint.

"It's intrusive." It's a dated argument but has received a bit more shelf life due to recent data-protection legislation. Some companies are afraid that if the content they serve is "too" personalized, customers might get paranoid about how their data is used, making them more likely to unsubscribe and less likely to engage or convert.

But we know now that the majority of consumers say it's critical for companies to provide a personalized experience. Additionally, over half will switch brands if a company doesn't personalize their communications. Research shows that most consumers are willing to share their personal data with brands in exchange for tailored discounts, offers, content, or perks. A significant portion of the population sees value in exchanging their data for a more personalized experience, as long as they get clear value from it.

"It's a trend." Personalization's rise in popularity is often mistaken for a fleeting trend, yet its deep-rooted benefits for tailoring individual customer experiences are undeniable and substantial. This misconception overlooks the transformative impact of unified solutions, which have liberated critical customer behavior data from the confines of isolated systems, making it increasingly actionable. Today's sophisticated machine learning algorithms enable the aggregation and analysis of customer data in real time, allowing businesses to offer optimally customized experiences to each individual. This approach has demonstrated a direct correlation with enhanced business profitability.

Personalization is establishing itself as a cornerstone of digital strategies across various industries. It's moving beyond being a transient trend toward becoming a universally recognized and essential practice. This shift indicates personalization's evolution into a fundamental, omnipresent component of modern business operations and highlights its lasting value and significant potential to drive growth.

"It's a tactic." Customizing the *|FNAME|* in the body of an email is a tactic. Deploying advanced targeting, behavioral messaging, dynamic content, product recommendations, and on-site/in-app personalization is a full-fledged discipline that involves lots of moving parts.

A/B testing has long been relied on for producing massive uplifts in conversion and revenue for those who identify the best possible variation for 51+ percent of site visitors. But we need experiments that consider the unique conditions that comprise the other 49 percent.

With various potential applications that transcend marketing channels, personalization is at the top of the food chain when it comes to enhancing the customer experience as one-to-one supersedes a one-to-many approach.

The greater the investment in operationalizing around personalization, the greater the result from ensuring the most relevant content gets served to the right audience segments.

"It's too involved." This is a natural argument after learning that personalization requires a lot of time, effort, and resources; managers will need answers to grapple with each and keep the conversation moving. Thankfully, employing the right personalization solution helps automate elements of a business's existing workflows, particularly in data analysis and testing/optimization, and makes it easier for teams to create experiences and launch and scale campaigns more quickly.

When coordinating a new set of responsibilities, many organizations leverage existing talent to tackle fresh potential use cases and applications. In some cases, project ownership and responsibility move from one team to another, where current org members can come together to oversee personalization activities (we'll go over team structure options in just a few pages).

Solidifying Its Worth

Because personalization can require a significant change in cultural mindset, don't be discouraged if the buy-in process doesn't move as quickly as you'd like—continued education and conversation around the vision and practice are necessary to foster commitment.

Good things will come with time, patience, and persistence. But it's essential to identify and communicate the financial impact of the personalization program to leadership.

Research has found that the value of personalization is exponential: Brands can expect to see ~5 to 25 percent of revenue driven by personalization, depending on a program's maturity. From improved revenue to increased conversions, deeper engagement, higher average order values, reduced customer acquisition costs, and boosted media efficiency, personalization can affect vital financial metrics within various industries.

As you begin testing and building out your road map, you'll be able to measure results and report back to key stakeholders on your progress.

TRANSMISSION FROM YOUR FUTURE:

FOCUS ON IMPACT IN MEASUREMENT AND COMMUNICATION

Adhering to a process for regularly circulating test results with relevant teams and executive leadership is one signal of the most advanced personalization programs. Get into the practice early and see your program's impact multiply.

To effectively measure the impact of personalization, you should utilize a global control group, where a small subset of customers are intentionally not exposed to any personalized content or experiences as part of a controlled experiment. This group's interactions and behaviors are monitored alongside those of customers who do receive personalized content. By comparing the two groups' outcomes, businesses can measure the real impact of personalization efforts on key performance indicators such as engagement, conversion rates, and customer loyalty. This method provides a clear, unbiased assessment of personalization's effectiveness, allowing companies to make data-driven decisions to optimize their strategies.

DETERMINING THE CORRECT
ORGANIZATIONAL STRUCTURE

Now that you've enlisted suitable champions to help evangelize personalization within your organization, it's time to execute. Your success relies heavily on selecting the right talent, orchestrating relationships and collaboration between departments and stakeholders, prioritizing initiatives, and then baking personalization into current workflows and processes to ease implementation.

Personalization challenges organizational communication uniquely, demanding tight collaboration across technical, business, and creative teams. Every department, from brand to acquisition and development, must contribute.

A dedicated executive sponsor or senior management team is crucial for breaking down silos, setting clear objectives, and guiding how departments collaborate. Without a clear understanding of their roles and personalization's impact, programs risk losing momentum. These leaders must encourage a "fail fast, learn fast" mindset, viewing every campaign as a learning opportunity—even those that don't yield the expected results. So long, of course, as everyone follows best practices to reach the statistical significance required to make informed decisions about personalization experiments and tests.

Giving teams the space to experiment fosters acceptance and commitment, ultimately accelerating the ability to launch campaigns and maximize performance. Bogging teams down with burdensome requirements limits this and, by definition, waters down a team's creativity, obstructing powerful experiences from positively affecting the business.

Without getting into the rigorous process teams must adopt to create effective and efficient personalization campaigns, you need certain functions to take an experience from A to Z. Starting with ideation and moving to prioritization, mock-up, development, segmentation, experience setup, quality assurance and launch, all the way through validating the results of the experience.

Individuals from various departments—product development, marketing/merchandising, and optimization/analytics—will roll up to an executive to form a unified (all housed under one department) or cross-functional personalization team (with each role sitting in separate departments). For best results, have one key stakeholder under the executive who "owns" the personalization program and coordinates collaboration between the various needed functions.

Key Functions of Any Personalization Team

Individuals may not be dedicated to personalization full-time*

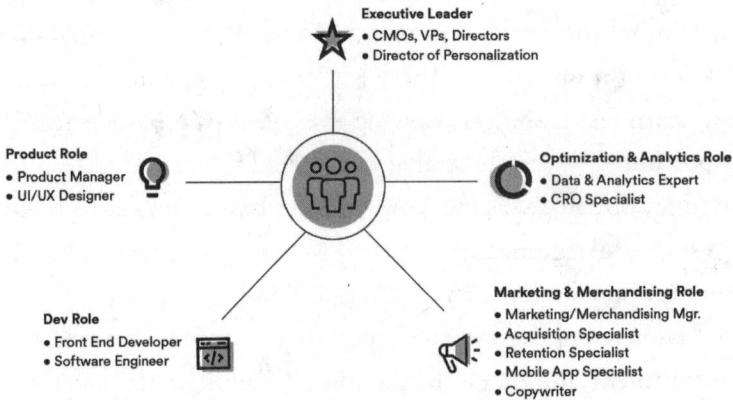

Executive Leader
- CMOs, VPs, Directors
- Director of Personalization

Product Role
- Product Manager
- UI/UX Designer

Optimization & Analytics Role
- Data & Analytics Expert
- CRO Specialist

Dev Role
- Front End Developer
- Software Engineer

Marketing & Merchandising Role
- Marketing/Merchandising Mgr.
- Acquisition Specialist
- Retention Specialist
- Mobile App Specialist
- Copywriter

A straightforward framework of the key roles found within any functional, well-oiled personalization team

Within each function, you can sub in various suitable titles to meet the role requirement based on an organization's needs and available resources. What's more important are the jobs individuals will perform, their impact on the workflow, and, ultimately, the customer experience.

These are the critical roles within a personalization team and their specific duties. Each of these roles has the freedom to sit anywhere within the org:

LEADER	TECHNICAL EXECUTORS
Strategic alignment Stakeholder coordination Prioritized campaign approval/review Communication of results	**Developer** Estimation of implementation efforts Necessary code implementation Experiment release QA

BUSINESS OPERATORS	CHANNEL OWNERS
Optimization & Analytics Role Insight gathering from existing data Insight activation Impact evaluation and documentation **Product Role** Idea generation In-platform campaign deployment Adjustment and creation of new tests **CX Expert** Identifies relevant segments Develops creative or experiences Reimagines the customer journey	**Acquisition Specialist** Media buying CR improving A/B test idea generation **Retention Specialist** Coordination with email Design of triggered email experiences Loyalty program engagement design **Mobile App Owner** Mobile app experience generation Mobile app integration across the journey

CREATIVE GURUS	
UI Designer	Experiences, banners, and template design
Copywriter	Message crafting and content article generation

In an ideal world, cross-functional experts would unite to oversee activities and implement ideas under one department. But this setup may not be universally adaptable because companies possess varying budgets, resources, and talent. Each role has the freedom to sit anywhere within the org, but many do not have to be dedicated to personalization full-time. But a dedicated owner for personalization is key to a program's long-term success.

Here are a few distinct team models your organization will likely implement during its personalization journey.

The Part-Time Model

One individual with an existing marketing/operations role spends a specific percentage of their time project managing experience-optimization efforts. They coordinate resources and activities across business teams to deliver campaigns. Technical resources are available for specific campaigns but require long lead times.

BENEFITS	CHALLENGES
The program receives consistent focus through part-time ownership	Extended execution timetables due to a lack of departmental representation
	Reduced interdepartmental expertise available to achieve maximum incrementality
	Limited execution capabilities without development resources

The Designated Owner Model

One individual is designated to manage A/B testing, optimization, or personalization efforts full-time. This ensures that campaigns are effectively orchestrated at the department level and that efforts are aligned behind centralized strategies and insights. Additionally, each business team involved has a point of contact within that area of expertise and is responsible for coordinating their deliverables.

BENEFITS	CHALLENGES
The program receives consistent focus through full-time ownership	Limited execution capabilities without dedicated development resources
Heightened program visibility through the creation of a new department	
Better collaboration and application of internal expertise	

The Dedicated Team Model

One individual owns personalization on a team of dedicated subject matter experts (SMEs), coordinating and delivering the program objectives. Member(s), which include business and technical experts, work cross-functionally to effectively deliver campaigns.

BENEFITS	CHALLENGES
The program receives consistent focus through full-time ownership	Increased expectations and demands to deliver incremental returns
Heightened program visibility through the creation of a new department	
Better collaboration and application of internal expertise	
Accelerated rate of deployment, effectiveness, and gains	
Development resources remove technical limitations	

It's important to note that KPI alignment for the program is critical regardless of which model you implement. KPIs should flow up to larger business objectives as well as involve all relevant stakeholders, fostering greater collaboration and commitment.

Now that you've built the proper team setup, you can move on to establishing a process around ideation, prioritization, campaign creation, execution, and analysis, helping personalization prosper across business units.

GET STRAIGHT TO THE SIGNAL: INTEGRATING PERSONALIZATION

BENEFITS

- Increases ROI, engagement, customer loyalty, and revenue.
- Creates a more relevant and engaging customer experience.

WHY IS IT IMPORTANT?

- Customers expect personalized experiences.
- It helps brands stand out from the competition.
- It allows brands to anticipate and address customer needs.

THE COST OF NOT PERSONALIZING

- Lost revenue and customers
- Inefficient marketing efforts
- Difficulty keeping up with competition

GETTING STARTED

- Find an executive sponsor: Get buy-in from a leader who understands the value of personalization.
- Define your vision: Create a clear plan for personalization across your organization.
- Build your team: Assemble a team with the skills and expertise to implement personalization.
- Start small: Begin with a few pilot projects and scale up as you see success.

Chapter Three

THE BUILD-OUT

✕ ✤ ✖ ✳

ACTIVATING PERSONALIZATION

Now that you've learned (or been refreshed on) the foundations of personalization and how to set up a culture of personalization within your organization, it's time to build out and effectively scale campaign creation. Broadly, your personalization approach will follow this methodology:

1. Analyze your data for insights and opportunities
2. Brainstorm ideas or concepts for testing
3. Define a hypothesis and matching KPI for each idea
4. Prioritize and plan for potential test ideas
5. Develop the intended customer experience
6. Evaluate and optimize

You'll continuously learn, adapt, and evolve your approach based on the data and insights you glean.

1. ANALYSIS

While businesses may share goals like increasing revenue, the effectiveness of personalization strategies can vary widely based on specific site and audience dynamics. To make data-driven decisions for your personalization road map, start by evaluating your analytics to find areas where high traffic coincides with poor performance, indicating inefficient spots. This approach can uncover your customers' underlying needs or desires, guiding you toward targeted improvements and more impactful personalization efforts. Identifying these pain points is a critical step in tailoring experiences that resonate with your audience and drive better outcomes.

2. IDEATION

Gather your core team to share knowledge, boost engagement, and break down silos. Leverage insights from data analysis to brainstorm and categorize new test ideas. This collaborative process facilitates the quick generation of concepts and highlights potential areas for experimentation you might otherwise miss. Organize your testing strategies into two main types: (1) content-related personalization, and (2) recommendations / merchandising strategies, which require a product data feed. This structured approach to ideation ensures a comprehensive exploration of avenues for enhancing personalization efforts.

Content-Related Personalization

The ultimate goal of personalization is to always show the most relevant information to each visitor, which will allow you to hook customers and move them toward achieving your KPIs. You can test banners, content, layouts, offers, overlays, emails, push notifications, and messaging.

Product Recommendations

Among personalization tactics, recommendations stand out for their profound impact, making them a popular choice from the onset and throughout the journey of personalization. For example, introducing a recommendation widget on product detail pages (PDPs) is an effective way to familiarize yourself with and assess basic personalization techniques. Recommendations on PDPs significantly contribute to direct revenue, sometimes representing 60–70 percent or more of a personalization program's total effect. This success is attributed to the high traffic and lower funnel position of PDPs, where customers are more inclined to move ahead with purchases, making it an ideal spot for product recommendations.

Expand the placement of recommendation widgets or campaigns to other strategic areas such as the home page, category pages, cart pages, navigation menus, and even overlays or pop-ups. Encourage creative thinking about locations that can expedite customer goals more effectively. Tailor your approach by experimenting with various strategies, layouts, and positions to discover the most effective solutions for your business. Consider leveraging pop-ups, null search results pages, themed landing pages, and emails to further enhance personalization.

Recommendation strategies provide the logic behind the item selection within your widget based on a particular algorithm (for example, the most popular items, items the customer viewed in the past, and so on). And much like there are lots of different types of personalized experiences a brand can deliver, there are also many recommendation strategies to experiment with.

When it comes to product recommendations, there are three major types of strategies teams can look to when crafting their plans:

1. Global Strategies

These strategies focus on general characteristics and trends across the customer base, offering recommendations relevant to a broader audience. As the home page is the main entry point, marketers often use these strategies to showcase to new site visitors.

Most Popular

Recommends top-selling products or most-viewed content. One popular recommendation strategy is to display "top items," or items ranked as "highly purchased" or "best." Items are scored based on the weighted sum of all interactions, such as purchases, adds-to-cart, and product views. The system favors recent interactions over historical ones and updates scores every time a data feed is synchronized.

As this strategy usually isn't based on hyperpersonalized customer data, it's beneficial when little to nothing is known about a customer or when a customer displays behavior that they are simply browsing around the site. It's also great for promoting your hottest items, helping your business stand out against your competition. It will assist with and enhance the product discovery experience, helping you market your brand and the popular merchandise it offers.

Additionally, using the "popular" recommendation strategy, brands can surface popular products to site visitors. Similar to the "most popular" strategy, products are scored based on the sum of all interactions before being served to customers. For example, once a brand identifies the top twenty-, fifty-, or hundred-plus products for sale on the site, it can use this strategy to display any five products in the cohort in a home page recommendation widget, rather than solely the five most popular products.

One other similar strategy is the more specific "most popular in category" strategy, which not only surfaces the most popular items but only includes items from a specified category. "Trending" can also be used to highlight products or content experiencing a surge in popularity or interest.

You can also filter by "newest arrivals," which showcases recently added products or content, and "seasonal picks," which curates recommendations based on seasonal trends and preferences.

2. Contextual Strategies

These strategies consider the current context of the customer, such as the product they're viewing or their browsing behavior, to suggest related or complementary items. These usually perform well on product detail pages or article pages.

Similarity

As its name would imply, widgets powered by a "similarity" strategy display products that resemble the item (or group of items) currently in view, factoring in the item's popularity. Complex algorithms are designed to ascertain the metrics— using categories and keywords provided from the data feed— resulting in a similarity "score" for each item. Then the products with the highest similarity scores are displayed to the customer.

While there are many applications for this strategy, one of the most efficient is to place a recommendation widget powered by the "similarity" strategy on a product detail page. Doing so will expose the site visitor not only to additional products but also to products they are likely interested in. Surfacing items similar to a product in view will potentially communicate a business's ability to understand what the customer is looking for, increasing the likelihood of driving a successful sale.

Product recommendations carry specific contextual strategies and can be good for product description pages. Also, if a "just added" recommendation widget can be deployed via pop-up after a customer adds an item to their cart, consider using these strategies to drive up your average order value, especially if you showcase products that are slightly cheaper than those in a customer's cart. It empowers customers to decide on additional products quickly, often resulting in upsells.

There is also the "visual similarity" approach, which utilizes deep learning to recommend items visually similar to the viewed product, catering to customer preferences beyond explicit descriptions. This typically works well on PDPs and add-to-cart pages.

Bought Together

Under this strategy, widgets display items that are frequently purchased together with the item currently in view. If your goal is to pad a visitor's cart with additional products, using this strategy presents upselling and cross-selling opportunities (that is, a car charger to go with a new smartphone, sandals for a pair of shorts, socks to go with a fresh pair of sneakers).

The system scores products based on the number of times they have been purchased together in the same transaction, demoting products that are typically purchased with many other items. Additionally, it recommends products that are strongly linked to one another rather than products that have an arbitrary connection to a popular product.

One popular way marketers employ this strategy is for a "complete your look" widget, which showcases a collection of products that complement one another. Additionally, when a visitor adds a product to their cart, this "bought together" strategy can upsell the customer, encouraging them to purchase another recommended product.

Viewed Together

This recommendation strategy is dependent on what product a customer is currently viewing. The system scores other items based on the number of times it has been viewed with the item in view in a single session. When an item is typically viewed with many different items, the system deems the connection weak, decreasing the likelihood of it being served as a recommendation.

3. Personalized Strategies.

Personalized recommendation strategies can leverage individual customer data to suggest items that cater to each customer's specific preferences, browsing, and purchasing history. These algorithms are typically used to target returning visitors, with some designed specifically for new visitors. You can deploy these strategies across pages and screens. Think about category pages displaying and automatically sorting relevant SKUs according to each customer's unique affinity profile and preferences.

Deep Learning

Self-training algorithms typically leverage recurrent neural networks to predict the next best item a customer will most likely engage with, based on other customers with similar browsing or purchasing history. These algorithms can also be designed to engage customers with relevant items from the very first page view.

Collaborative Filtering

One of the most popular recommendation strategies, collaborative filtering bases recommendations on similarities between different customers. The system analyzes the behavior of customers similar to a current customer—the items they've viewed, the products they've purchased, the items they've added to their carts—and recommends these products to other customers displaying similar preferences and behavior, on any page type.

TRANSMISSION FROM YOUR FUTURE:

LOOKING BEYOND COLLABORATIVE FILTERING

While collaborative filtering is a popular strategy in the market, research has found that "recently viewed" and "viewed together" algorithms consistently outperform it. Deep learning algorithms are rising in popularity for these use cases, such as those that identify the relationships between different items by looking at product interactions across the user base and recommending the next best item accordingly.

Affinity Based

Affinity-based strategies allow marketers to make compelling product recommendations when and to whom they matter most. As customers browse a site, interacting with various products, they are exposed to several product attributes, such as color, brand, style, and more. Recommender systems then use these interactions to identify and infer customer affinities and preferences, building rich profiles for each site visitor.

This strategy makes recommendations personalized to each individual customer. Affinity profiles feature a weighted score based on the correlation between customer interactions (number of views, add-to-carts, purchases, and so on) and the attributes of products they've interacted with. The system then bases its recommendations on these scores and can work in real time, detecting any preference changes. Often taking the form of a "Recommended for You" widget, this strategy is suitable for all page types.

Recently Viewed

When using this strategy, the system recommends the last items the current customer viewed, with the most recently viewed items appearing first. These recommendations are typically based on data from the last thirty days. A similar approach is the "viewed with recently viewed" strategy, which displays items that are typically viewed in the same session as the last items viewed by the current customer.

Last/Recent Purchase

This recommendation strategy specifically looks at the most recent purchase(s) a customer has made, typically within the last year. Ideal for encouraging repeat purchase behavior, it surfaces products a customer has purchased that may need to be replenished (such as pet food, makeup). A simple and straightforward strategy, it displays the most recently purchased product by a customer in a recommendation widget.

Bought With

When you onboard offline transaction data, you can leverage it to power smarter recommendations online. With the "purchased together offline" strategy, the system can recommend products that have been purchased together offline with the item currently in view on the site or app. The products displayed in these widgets are scored based on the number of times they have been purchased together in the same transaction, recommending products that are strongly linked to one another and demoting products that are typically purchased with many other items.

Similar to the offline recommendation strategy, a "purchased together online/offline" strategy—using offline transaction data—recommends products that have been purchased together either offline or online with the item currently being displayed.

When using "purchased with recently purchased," the recommender system looks at the last items purchased by the current customer, suggesting items that are usually bought together with these recent purchases. For example, when deployed on the home page, this strategy can show all visitors who have bought an item in the past week complementary items while they are still relevant.

Akin to the "purchased with recently purchased" strategy, the "purchased with last purchase" approach ensures all recommendations are based solely on the most recent purchase completed by the current customer.

Picking a Strategy: The optimal strategy for your business depends on various factors, including your product range, available customer data, and marketing goals. Often, a combination of different strategies proves most effective, allowing you to cater recommendations to diverse customer segments and contexts. By strategically employing these categories, you can leverage the power of personalization to create a more engaging and profitable shopping experience for your customers.

3. DEFINE HYPOTHESES AND KPIs

Now that you know roughly the options you can choose from, try and whittle down your options by hypothesizing changes to the site that may (hopefully) cause positive, desired outcomes based on the data (if available) and ideas generated thus far.

A good way to go about building a hypothesis would be to use the following statement and plug in the missing details:

IF we [proposed change to the site or digital experience] FOR [audience], THEN we will [affect KPI] BECAUSE [reason behind why we think the outcome will be positive].

TRANSMISSION FROM YOUR FUTURE:

MAXIMIZE EFFICACY THROUGH RECOMMENDATIONS TESTING

When evaluating the effectiveness of recommendation strategies, it's crucial to test multiple approaches not only against each other but also to include a control group for baseline comparison. This method allows for a comprehensive analysis if your initial assumptions are challenged. For instance, implementing

A/B testing where Strategy A and Strategy B are evaluated in the context of actual user interactions provides direct insights into their performance. Including a control group, where no recommendations are made, further clarifies the incremental impact of each strategy. This detailed approach ensures that decisions are data driven, enhancing the likelihood of selecting the most effective recommendation strategy based on empirical evidence.

Your hypotheses should not be confused with facts. Hypotheses are not facts but argued ideas based on data analysis and knowledge. They act as a starting point for the optimization process.

Hypotheses should be closely tied to the why, or goal, supporting the test because they are largely driven by the business's objectives and its online activities. It's important, therefore, to explore the desired outcomes of each launched experience. Set the right KPIs to understand impact over the long term. A good rule of thumb is to look at the next logical step in the funnel. For example, if you changed something on the home page, the next logical step would be the click-through rate or page views. Product view or add-to-cart would make sense for a product listing page, and revenue per customer for the cart itself.

4. PRIORITIZE AND PLAN

With all the excitement and speculation behind building experiences, it's easy to get carried away. But with any initiative, it's crucial to take the time to consider the estimated impact and effort of each initiative before pulling the trigger. Otherwise, you'll end up wasting valuable time and energy on campaigns that are unrealistic or offer little to no value to the business. And that can really hurt the long-term sustainability of a personalization program.

Use the methodology below to aid the decision-making process, measuring the ultimate outcome of each test being reviewed based on two factors: **Impact** and **Effort**.

IMPACT	EFFORT
Rated holistically, can be measured by high, medium, or low.	Rated holistically, can be measured by high, medium, or low.
Company objectives Time to impact Step in the purchase funnel Excitement Executive sponsor Reduced costs	Teams involved Code complexity Test definition

The time, effort, and resources required will largely depend on how mature an organization's personalization efforts are. But whatever the case, prioritizing these tests is key to reducing design and development cycles for the quick and effective implementation of campaigns. Because if the scope of the project doesn't match up with the test schedule, you'll miss deadlines and the customer information associated with a campaign will go stale, resulting in lower-impact results, not to mention a poor customer experience.

Using this prioritization matrix, a company can easily score, prioritize, and place the most valuable test ideas on a timeline for implementation.

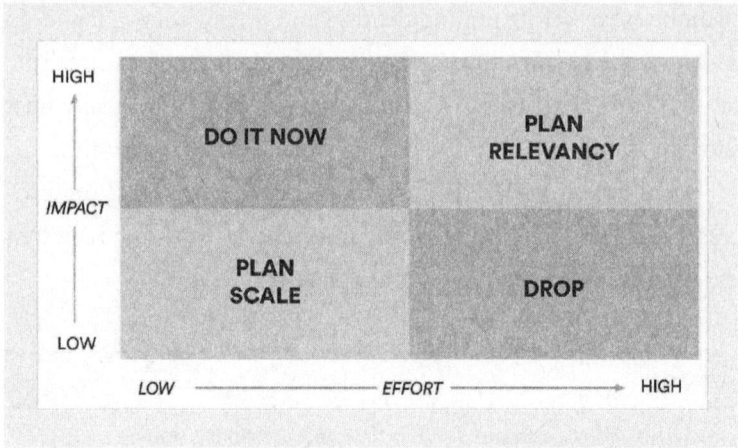

Impact vs. effort prioritization matrix

Once armed with a list of vetted ideas, you should define the specifics of each campaign in a test brief. This document will be populated by some of the information already established in previous steps, while also outlining important considerations for implementation, such as the parameters of the test, segmentation strategies, timeline, and duration.

Key stakeholders should work together in the creation of each brief, using it as a point of reference for everything to do with execution: the agreement on the approach, coordination of schedules, and reinforcing responsibilities through launch, validation, and optimization phases. Then, the build officially begins.

5. DEVELOP THE INTENDED EXPERIENCE

Using all of the information collected in previous steps as a guide, expertise from both visual and technical functions must now align to create the customer experience itself. Typically, the following workflow is adopted to first mock-up or "stage" how the final campaign will look:

1. Copy and calls-to-action are drafted.
2. Designs are mocked up.
3. Specs are built.

This alone can take weeks, sometimes months depending on the efficiency of workflows, which is why building a culture of experimentation is so important to an organization's ability to scale a personalization program. Alternatively, using templates in this part of campaign creation can reduce the design and development cycles typically associated with failure to launch on time.

Once an experience is developed, it will then typically go into a review process to ensure it meets all the agreed-upon requirements. During this test for quality assurance:

- any kinks in functionality are noted,
- updates to the experience are made, and
- approval for final implementation is received.

Of course, further quality assurance cycles may be necessary.

6. EVALUATE, OPTIMIZE, REPEAT

Just as important to the success of a campaign as all the work that led up to the launch is the close monitoring, analyzing, and optimizing that takes place after the launch.

It's no secret that human intuition is naturally subject to ego and bias, which is why marketers adopted the scientific method of A/B testing for evaluating and serving experiences instead of relying on gut-based decisions that produce subpar results and quickly diminishing returns.

The premise of A/B testing is simple: compare two (or more) different versions of something (creative elements, copy, layouts, algorithms) to see which performs better and then deploy the winner to all customers for the most optimal overall experience. A/B testing allows teams to experiment and improve different areas and experiences across the site, native app, email, or any other digital channel and then continuously optimize these features to drive incremental uplift in conversions and specific KPIs over time.

Personalization takes A/B testing a step further, providing the best experience at an audience or individual level.

A/B testing within personalization creates multiple experiences targeted at different audiences and multiple variations within each that can be A/B tested. Machine learning analyzes the performance of each variation across every traffic segment in real time to determine the best-performing one and serve the most relevant content to select audience groups.

By definition, classic A/B testing uses manual traffic allocation where traffic is split evenly between variations until a single winner is declared. The first thing you will need to do in order to test your hypothesis and analyze your results with accuracy is to set up your variations and your control group. Allocating 50 percent of each audience's traffic to your new variation and 50 percent to your control will give you clear insight into how your test variation performs across your audiences. This method minimizes room for error and, if it runs long enough or with enough data, can provide you with statistically significant results.

TRANSMISSION FROM YOUR PERSONALIZED FUTURE:

OPTIMIZE TRAFFIC ALLOCATION METHODS

Sometimes you will seek to run a campaign for a short time, perhaps for a Black Friday promotion that will only run for a few days. In these cases, you'd leverage a multiarmed bandit method. This approach dynamically allocates more traffic to the best-performing variation in real time. Unlike traditional A/B testing, which splits traffic evenly regardless of performance, multiarmed bandit optimizes for the highest success during the campaign by quickly identifying and leveraging the winning variation. This method ensures that your campaign capitalizes on the most effective strategy, maximizing potential returns within a limited time frame.

Measure the Impact of Campaigns

Determining the optimal duration for an experiment is crucial to mitigate the risk of false positives and solidify the reliability of a campaign's outcomes, which depend on both the sample size and the variation complexity. While attributing KPI shifts to specific interventions is appealing for bolstering a personalization initiative, it's prudent to await results that are both statistically significant and repeatable before enacting changes or broadcasting successes.

To ensure robust results, test durations may vary. You should also account for unique business impacts and seasonality. It's also essential to analyze a variety of metrics, including but not limited to the "probability to be best," which estimates a variation's long-term performance advantage, incorporating factors like sample size through a Bayesian approach. This metric, alongside others, assists in discerning the most effective variation in A/B tests, with statistical calculations starting once a foundational data threshold is met, which may adjust based on the specific experiment design and objectives.

Convention recommends identifying a winning variation when the "probability to be best" achieves a 95 percent confidence level. But in scenarios of diminished campaign traffic, prolonging the test to accommodate a lower confidence threshold may be more appropriate.

Uplift measurement, representing the performance differential between a test variation and the control group, is another critical metric. For instance, an uplift of 25 percent is observed if a test variation achieves a revenue per customer of five dollars compared to four dollars for the control.

You will also want to look at how the experiment variations performed for different customer segments.

In the example on page 63 highlighting an experiment introducing star ratings on product landing pages (PLPs), you can see that the test variation produced an uplift across the primary metric we set up for the test (in this case, purchases per customer). The test variation has not yet been declared as the "winner." Despite not reaching true statistical significance, there are clear indicators that the test is producing an uplift and has a 79 percent probability to be best.

Purchases _Primary Metric_					
Variation ↑	Users	Purchase	Purchase/ Users	Uplift	Probability to be Best
Control Group	14,904	1,301	0.0873	Baseline	21%
Show PLP Reviews	14,872	1,355	0.0911	+4.4%	79%

Different experiment scenarios will merit varying levels of treatment in terms of confidence thresholds—look for clear performance indicators to make the most informed decisions

If you are personalizing by audience group, you'll likely see a clear winning variation for each segment. At this point, you can discontinue the losing variations, continue running with the winner, gather data about why that variation won for that audience, and unlock further personalization opportunities.

TRANSMISSIONS FROM YOUR FUTURE:

WHEN LOSING VARIATIONS END UP AS WINNERS

While a specific variation may "lose" the A/B test, the test actually just identifies a new microsegment that prefers this variation. For example, say you launched a simple test to determine the best copy for a new hero banner campaign, consisting of a control group and treatment variation. The results revealed that the control group won unequivocally, while the variation significantly hurt overall performance. But 30 percent of those who viewed the banner did respond well to it. While this variation "lost" the A/B test, it was still able to be served to the 30 percent that preferred it—an opportunity for better personalization and a foundation to test and learn more about that group of individuals.

Turning Insights into Action

Most experimentation solutions offer an audience breakdown that shows how the results of a test differ when segmenting the traffic by different audiences. Analyze how the test performs across your different segments to gain a deeper understanding of your audiences and begin building campaigns that better serve the needs of each group.

Write down a few notes for each winning variation: Why do you think it performed well, especially compared to the other variations? Keeping track of this over time will give you critical insights into what motivates your audience segments. Once you've analyzed your data and drawn conclusions about how the results relate to key behavior differences, you can begin to set up your next test to further act on your learnings and deliver a more personalized experience to your customers.

Analyzing and recording this data over time will not only strengthen your personalization program, but it will empower all areas of your business and help other departments become more strategic in their interactions with different customer groups on other channels, including paid ads, physical assets, and so much more. Customers need to see a message several times, in several places, before they take action—and identifying what messages work best can help elevate all marketing initiatives.

In the example below, low- and medium-intent customers increased purchases by nearly 6 percent when star reviews were shown on PLPs, indicating a preference for additional social proof. But high-intent customers favored a simpler PLP for a streamlined shopping experience. As a result, we'd show star ratings to low- and medium-intent customers for trust and engagement, while offering high-intent customers a cleaner

Purchase Per User	Control	Show PLP Reviews	Delta
Low Intent	0.052	0.055	5%
Medium Intent	0.146	0.153	5%
High Intent	0.232	0.220	-5%

RPU	Control	Show PLP Reviews	Delta
Low Intent	$9.14	$9.83	8%
Medium Intent	$26.13	$28.78	10%
High Intent	$47.95	$43.86	-9%

AOV	Control	Show PLP Reviews	Delta
Low Intent	$176.43	$179.43	2%
Medium Intent	$179.34	$187.63	5%
High Intent	$206.95	$199.56	-4%

Pageviews	Control	Show PLP Reviews	Delta
Low Intent	6.97	7.08	2%
Medium Intent	11.70	11.80	1%
High Intent	17.30	16.20	-6%

Experiment results unlock deeper insight into the preferences among different intent level-based audiences

PLP layout to maintain their preference for a straightforward purchase process.

Unlock Potential with Continuous Testing

You've created a better site experience for your audiences, so, technically, your testing could end here. But by testing your winning variation against other iterations—phrasing, design, calls-to-action—you can continue homing in on the best site experience and ensure that your visitors always encounter the best, most relevant content for them. This will lead to more revenue and engagement over time.

IT TAKES A VILLAGE

A successful program needs continued support, proper education across the organization, and the right talent, culture, and processes. Those who invest in building an ecosystem around their efforts are always more effective.

Naturally, over time, any program will fluctuate, adapting to the needs of the organization. And each time a team works their way through the experience-building cycles previously, processes and workflows will become more efficient, creating a well-oiled machine that brings scalable and impactful personalization results to the entire company.

PERSONALIZATION METHODOLOGIES AND TOOLS

You can experiment with many different methodologies and tools within each step of the previously defined process. Here, we share two that have worked for brands across industries and geographies: the Primary Audiences Approach and Evergreen Personalization Zones.

THE PRIMARY AUDIENCES APPROACH

The Primary Audiences framework empowers teams to address the needs of different customer groups in a comprehensive, scalable, and repeatable way. When implemented, the framework creates a waterfall effect of richer and more consistent audience learnings, improved targeting and testing strategies, uplifts in business KPIs, and incremental revenue growth.

By first identifying valuable and profitable customer segments, marketers can delve deeper into personalizing experiences for individuals within these segments. This layered approach ensures that personalization efforts are grounded in an understanding of broader customer groups, thereby enhancing the effectiveness of targeting and relevance of communications. Once chosen, your Primary Audiences won't change frequently, even if your business does. So it's important to be thoughtful and take your time when identifying these core groups.

The criteria are as follows:

1. Define your audiences based on a clear, meaningful, and high-impact segmentation principle.

2. Keep your key audiences to a minimum and mutually exclusive to avoid overlap where it makes sense.

3. Together, audiences should add up to a meaningful portion of your overall traffic.

Let's dive into each criterion further.

Principle #1: *Define your audiences based on a clear, meaningful, and high-impact segmentation principle.*

The segmentation principle entails establishing Primary Audience groups that directly align with high-impact segments relevant to your business. These Primary Audiences should be defined based on factors such as intent level, affinity, customer types, or a combination of segmentation rules. Our experience working with diverse businesses across various industries reveals nuances in how different markets and sectors define their Primary Audience types. Here are some common examples for your inspiration:

- **Intent:** Segments may include low, medium, high intent.
- **Stage of Funnel:** Segments may include distinct buyer personas such as browser, researcher, and decider.
- **Customer Type:** Segments can be based on customer criteria such as subscriber versus nonsubscriber, B2B versus B2C, purchase value tiering, or loyalty member status.
- **Level of Knowledge:** Segments may include beginner, enthusiast, professional.
- **Affinity Audiences:** Segments can be based on real-time and historical site browsing data to determine customer interests and level of engagement.

- **Empathy Audiences:** Segments can be based on real-time and historical cues to determine users' states of mind and emotional needs.

An increasingly popular segmentation approach, reflecting evolving consumer behavior, involves categorizing audiences based on low, medium, and high purchase intent. Here are some characteristics you might observe with each audience:

LOW INTENT	MEDIUM INTENT	HIGH INTENT
Unfamiliar with site's offering or brand	Some familiarity with the brand	Has a good sense of what the brand offers
Limited time on site and minimal browsing	Might be deciding between offers	Understands what to shop for
Has not added any items to cart or submitted any forms	May have signed up for email or loyalty membership	Hasn't found the right product yet or needs a final push
	Has added an item to cart but not yet purchased	Lots of behavioral data from site activity
		Further along the funnel

TRANSMISSION FROM YOUR FUTURE:

IDENTIFY YOUR PRIMARY AUDIENCE SEGMENTS

While commonly used segmentation principles like intent are valuable, every business has its own intricacies. Rely on your deep understanding of customer behaviors and your business's

distinct perspective to uncover the Primary Audience segments
that resonate most effectively with your brand.

Once you've selected a segmentation principle, it's crucial to apply it consistently across your personalization program. Introducing additional segmentation principles can lead to audience fragmentation and dilute the effectiveness of your targeting efforts. Sticking to a single segmentation principle ensures clarity and coherence in your Primary Audience groups, guaranteeing exclusivity across your site traffic and providing a reliable baseline for your personalization strategy.

To develop a targeted plan for segmentation, it's essential to understand the characteristics of each segment and identify any significant differences between them. Adopting a single behavioral segmentation principle enables you to keep your strategy dynamic and focused on current customer actions rather than static concepts derived from past behavior that may become outdated. This approach also brings clarity to audience distinctions, allowing you to tailor experiences more effectively. Moreover, it fosters alignment among your team and other stakeholders involved in personalization efforts, facilitating executive buy-in and ensuring ongoing program support.

Principle #2: *Keep your key audiences to a minimum and mutually exclusive to avoid overlap where it makes sense.*
While numerous segmentation principles exist, it's crucial to prioritize simplicity. Scalability becomes paramount in resource-constrained environments. In most scenarios, avoiding overlap

among audiences enables effective targeting, analysis, and optimization of primary segments. But there are individuals who can be both "in love" and "curious" shoppers, so it's important to keep this in mind when building your strategy. A recommended starting point is three or four key audiences. Restricting Primary Audiences ensures scalable and repeatable segmentation, essential for long-term learning and institutionalization. Additionally, ensure that site visitors qualify for only one Primary Audience segment at any given time.

Principle #3: *Together, audiences should add up to a meaningful portion of your overall traffic.*

When your audiences encompass nearly 100 percent of your website traffic, or a substantial portion that directly influences your business revenue, you can discern the efficacy of strategies and campaigns in transitioning customers between segments. Once your audience segments are established, you can align your program road map and analysis accordingly. This framework serves as a cornerstone for future ideation, execution, and evaluation.

Personalizing to Everyone for Maximum Efficiency

The goal of personalization is to deliver greater relevance on the whole versus enhancing experiences for small pockets of traffic. Let's say, for example, a team decides to move forward with three Primary Audiences, one for each intent level (low, medium, and high). While altogether these buckets may account for close to 100 percent of visitors, the high-intent audience might make up only 3–5 percent of the overall traffic. While considered a microsegment, it allows you to track segment gains and understand what other strategies are contributing to its growth. If you targeted only this microsegment, you could track what works best for this high-performing segment, but you couldn't identify what strategies or campaigns work toward growing this segment. You'd be optimizing results, not pipeline.

While the Pareto Principle, famously articulated by Italian economist Vilfredo Pareto, suggests that 80 percent of effects stem from 20 percent of causes, many modern businesses find themselves in a paradigm where an even smaller minority drives significant outcomes. This evolution beyond the traditional 80/20 rule underscores the necessity of pinpointing opportunities to further optimize already high-value conversion rates.

A recent engagement audit conducted by our product team revealed a striking reality for the executives of a major media brand: Merely 2 percent of users were responsible for 50 percent of the site's total page views. Similarly, for a billion-dollar retail client, a mere 1 percent of customers were driving a staggering 67 percent of its annual revenue.

Consider this scenario: If only 0.5 percent of your traffic contributes to 25 percent of your revenue, it warrants a focused effort to optimize and personalize for this microsegment. While seizing such opportunities is essential, integrating them into your Primary Audience strategy allows you to translate segment wins into broader insights applicable throughout the customer journey.

Putting the Concept into Practice

Now it's your turn. Let's walk through this process together and brainstorm your business's Primary Audience groups.

First, ask yourself: What is your business's primary site KPI? Is it the number of conversions? New accounts opened? Average order value? Chats with an agent? Applications to a credit card?

Loyalty or membership program sign-ups? Your KPI will vary depending on your industry and particular business goals, so take some time to think this through.

Next, dig into some data. Find out which customers have already completed the main KPI event. What can you observe about the behavior of these customers? For example, did most of them come from a single traffic source? How many times did they visit your page, and which pages did they view? Do they have accounts? Have they achieved particular milestones? As you look at the behavior history of this group of customers, keep your main KPI in mind. What is the most common behavior in this group that indicates that the KPI will occur? The idea is that you should pinpoint not just the KPI behavior, but the one that precedes it. For example, if your main KPI is conversions, you may find that the number of page views is a solid indicator of a customer's likelihood to convert.

After analyzing the data, select the customer behavior that is the most likely indicator of achieving your KPI. Now, use your chosen behavior to build Primary Audience groups defined by a single segmentation principle. This step is where general advice becomes less practical than an example, as the logic here will depend heavily on your business.

So let's continue the previous example. Say that this is your business:

- Your main KPI is the number of conversions.
- You determine that the main behavior leading to conversion is page views.
- So it's reasonable to say that page views indicate a visitor's intent to convert.

Therefore, in a very simplistic way, intent may be your segmentation principle for your Primary Audience groups, and you'll use page views to break down traffic into main intent-based segments.

TRANSMISSION FROM YOUR FUTURE:

AUDIENCE STRATEGY DEVELOPMENT IS A TEAM EFFORT

During the brainstorming process, it's invaluable to seek input from various stakeholders. Identifying the optimal Primary Audiences may not always follow a linear path, but the collaborative effort yields rich business insights that are indispensable in the long run. Engaging with colleagues across departments brings diverse perspectives to the table, fostering a holistic understanding of customer behaviors and preferences. Moreover, involving different team members ensures that the chosen Primary Audiences resonate with all facets of the business, enhancing alignment and buy-in for personalized strategies and initiatives.

Once you know your segmentation principle and what behavior you'll use to break down your groups, you can start actively building your audiences in your personalization tool. Start with the smallest group first and work your way through the rest of the site traffic from there. In this example, perhaps the first Primary Audience group is "high intent," and it is defined as "visitors who view page X, Y, or Z at least three times within a thirty-day period."

Once you've segmented your audiences, review approximately how much of your site traffic falls into this Primary Audience group. While not all Primary Audience groups will be the same size, remember that together they should cover all of your traffic.

It's okay if your Primary Audiences aren't perfect on the first try. Remember, there is no single "correct" answer, and you can refine your segments as you gain more business insights.

TRANSMISSION FROM YOUR FUTURE:

HOW A LEADING GOLF RETAILER PUT PERSONALIZATION

INTO PRACTICE WITH PRIMARY AUDIENCES

Specializing in designing, manufacturing, and selling golf equipment, a US retailer wanted to craft an exceptional experience for its online shoppers. After identifying a correlation between conversions and the number of page views, its team decided to build and analyze a set of audiences based on low, medium, and high intent. Low was defined as the customer visiting fewer than a dozen pages, and high was when a customer visited more than two dozen.

Breaking down site visitors according to intent level revealed a few key insights about how different degrees of knowledge affected purchase decisions for the company's golf equipment:

Higher intent customers knew the drill, preferring more technical details and brand-specific product messaging, while low-intent customers often browsed according to "player type" and needed more education on specific products.

Using this info, the golf retailer was able to optimize its campaigns at the audience level. Specific category page messaging was designed and served to educate and drive purchases among low-intent customers. For example, a variation served on a Player Performance category page under Iron Sets included messaging that said "Trouble beating your buddies? Look AND play better on the golf course with player performance irons." This approach allowed the brand to more deeply understand each segment's behavior and yield even greater returns.

EVERGREEN PERSONALIZATION ZONES

It's recommended to implement a handful of Evergreen Personalization Zones at the beginning of a brand's personalization journey. These visible, high-traffic spots on your website function as "billboards" where you can test different content, like your unique selling propositions and educational resources. They are Evergreen Zones because you will strategically and continually test what is the most relevant content to show each audience group.

Common Evergreen Zones to choose from include (but are not limited to):

- Home page hero banners
- Home page containers (about two or three content pieces)
- PLP banners
- Footer components
- Global banners
- Mobile or desktop navigation pane banners
- Landing pages

Why is it so important to establish these zones as your Evergreen testing sites? One, if your developers and other departments agree that these areas should not be touched, then you remove the risk of a test malfunctioning. Two, if you secure buy-in from executives for regular access to these zones, then you can run tests and personalization campaigns consistently.

Evergreen Personalization Zones from left to right: hero banner and two home page containers, a product listing page banner, and a "billboard" in the site's navigation

DEFINING YOUR UNIQUE VALUE PROPOSITIONS

In terms of brainstorming copy and calls-to-action for your Ever-green Personalization Zones, it might help to do a value proposition exercise. You may already have some understanding or assumptions about what is important to your customers, but a successful person-alization program requires more than just assumptions.

It is critical to thoughtfully lay out the unique selling proposi-tions of your brand, agree on these as an organization, and then build a testing strategy accordingly to determine which points perform the best with your different audience segments. This data will inform many other decisions across the organization and can lead to a significant uplift in key metrics over time.

Step One: Brainstorm

Building a list of unique selling propositions (USPs) will benefit you by serving as a repository of ideas to test content, messag-ing, images, and more. It will also allow you to track the perfor-mance of each USP over time and give you important insights about what does (and doesn't) matter to your customers in each segment.

In the brainstorming phase, we recommend opening up a spreadsheet and starting with a list of the important aspects of your brand that you think matter to customers. Think of your assets in the following categories: features, selling points, and key information.

Features

A feature is an element on your website or app that a visitor can in-teract with. In general, they enhance the shopping experience and can increase product discovery. Some other examples of common features include:

- Virtual try-on
- In-store appointment booking
- Product finder quizzes
- Location finders
- Virtual stylist chat (different from a call center)
- Calculators or quote builders

Identifying the features that are most important to your brand and are most important to site visitors will help you clean up landing pages and provide a more streamlined experience.

What: The brand's unique assets	Primary Audience Segments		
Assets	Low Intent	Medium Intent	High Intent
Features			
Automatic renewal each month			
Option to pause			
Coffee selections matched to your preferences			
Selling Points			
Free shipping			
Discover beans from small roasters			
Higher quality for the same price as the grocery store			
Key Information			
Partnered with 200+ small roasters around the country			
High satisfaction rating from customers			
Featured in popular press			

A sample spreadsheet populated with the unique selling propositions that may appeal to customers of a (fictional) coffee subscription company

Selling Points

Identify the unique information that would compel a visitor to purchase from your company over a competitor's. These points will differ by industry, of course, but here are some examples that may look familiar:

- Generous return policy
- Long warranty
- Option to split payments
- Fit or durability
- Eco-friendly/sustainable
- Competitive quote rates
- Loyalty savings program
- Capstone products (key items your brand is well-known for)

Key Information

Closely related to the selling points is other key information that a customer might want to know when deciding to make a purchase. Again, key information will differ by industry and by brand, but some common examples include:

- Brand or product awards
- Endorsements
- Customer reviews
- Social proof (such as "trending on TikTok")

If you're struggling to identify unique selling propositions, try auditing the website from the perspective of a customer. Consider additional insights that your business knows, such as the highest-performing ads, the social posts that have received the most engagement, and the emails that have had the highest click-through rates. Read through customer reviews to find out what people love.

Your initial list might be extensive, so it's important to narrow down the selling propositions as much as possible. Remember, at this step, you simply want to define a few critical points that you can immediately test for each audience group. As you gather data about which points perform the best, you can eliminate some selling propositions and add in others.

TRANSMISSION FROM YOUR FUTURE:
A BRAND'S VISION AND OBJECTIVES ARE NEVER RUSHED

Take your time with this step and strive to secure buy-in from other departments whenever feasible. Establishing a cohesive and shared understanding of your brand's assets is pivotal for streamlining the path to personalization and extracting valuable insights from your testing strategies. By garnering support from various departments, you foster collaboration and ensure that personalized initiatives align seamlessly with the overarching brand vision and objectives.

Step Two: Define This Information by Audience.

Once you have the list of your brand's assets, create a first hypothesis about which information will be most relevant to your different audience segments.

Regardless of how you are thinking about your audiences, it is important to form a hypothesis about how important you think each brand message will be for each. In the example sheet

What: The brand's unique assets	Primary Audience Segments		
Assets	Low Intent	Medium Intent	High Intent
Features			
Automatic renewal each month	n/a	n/a	Somewhat important
Option to pause	Somewhat important	Very important	n/a
Coffee selections matched to your preferences	Somewhat important	**Extremely important**	Very important
Selling Points			
Free shipping	**Extremely important**	n/a	n/a
Discover beans from small roasters	n/a	Very important	**Extremely important**
Higher quality for the same price as the grocery store	**Extremely important**	Somewhat important	n/a
Key Information			
Partnered with 200+ small roasters around the country	n/a	Somewhat important	**Extremely important**
High satisfaction rating from customers	Somewhat important	**Extremely important**	Very important
Featured in popular press	n/a	n/a	Very important

Defined assets across categories have been ranked by importance for each of this fictional coffee company's audiences

above, we specified this with somewhat, very, extremely, or not applicable for each line item.

A hypothesis like this one is highly useful and should be the foundation for your comprehensive testing strategies. As data comes in, you can update your sheet accordingly to track which selling points are actually performing the best. The results may surprise you.

TRANSMISSION FROM YOUR FUTURE:

IDENTIFY GAPS BETWEEN HYPOTHESIS AND OUTCOME

Analyzing the disparity between your hypothesis and the actual content performance yields invaluable, data-driven

insights. These insights are instrumental in understanding consumer behavior, benefiting the entire company and serving as
a road map for your personalization program.

Taking It a Step Further

An exercise like this one can be useful for more than just your brand's selling points; it can also help you identify key differentiators between products and product categories, and it can help you find out which products perform best for your different audience segments.

Once you feel comfortable with your overall brand, try applying this exercise to your product categories or individual products.

What: The brand's unique assets	Primary Audience Segments		
Assets	Low Intent	Medium Intent	High Intent
Features			
2 minute application process	n/a	Somewhat important	n/a
Redeem points through an exclusive travel site with unique discounts	n/a	n/a	Extremely important
Selling Points			
1,000x bonus points on sign up	Very important	Very important	Extremely important
3x points on transportation and hotels	Very important	Extremely important	Extremely important
1x points on every purchase	n/a	Somewhat important	n/a
No interest for the first year	Somewhat important	Very important	Somewhat important
Key Information			
#1 travel card as rated by press	Extremely important	Very important	Very important
235 applications in the past week	n/a	Somewhat important	Very important
No annual fee	Very important	Extremely important	Extremely important

Unique selling points for singular products of a fictional travel credit card include a hypothesis about which will perform best for each audience segment

Step Three: Build Different Content Variations

Next, take your chosen unique selling propositions and create the content that will populate your variations. How will you sell each point to your customer? For example, if your selling point is "the product is high quality," it is rarely enough to simply state that it is high quality. How might you prove this? Can you describe the materials, showcase a customer review, or reference an award?

TRANSMISSION FROM YOUR FUTURE:

BE CONSISTENT UNTIL YOU'VE GATHERED ADEQUATE INTEL

In the early stages, don't worry so much about your content zone's design and placement. It may be a good idea to stick with the same template and placement so you can focus on the messaging—this will give you accurate data about how the actual messages resonate with your customers. Over time, after you've gathered information about the best way to articulate and sell your relevant messages, you can then invest and test the design.

Doing this exercise will help you gain clarity on selling points, identify testing opportunities, and discover which messages resonate best with each audience, enabling you to optimize every single page on your site. This data creates a strong foundation for understanding your customers, paving the way for true one-to-one personalization.

GET STRAIGHT TO THE SIGNAL: ACTIVATING PERSONALIZATION

THE PRACTICAL STEPS FOR IMPLEMENTING PERSONALIZATION STRATEGIES

1. Analyze your data for insights and opportunities

- Start by analyzing website analytics to identify areas where high traffic coincides with low performance, revealing potential pain points.
- This data can guide targeted improvements and inform personalization efforts.

2. Ideation

- Gather your team: Brainstorm and categorize new test ideas leveraging the insights from data analysis.
- Organize your strategy: Structure your testing around content-related personalization and product recommendations, and choose strategies on factors like product range, customer data, and marketing goals. Consider a combination of strategies for diverse customer segments and contexts.
- Recommendations/merchandising: Requires product data feed.
  - Global strategies focus on broad customer trends, ideal for showcasing products to new visitors (for example, most popular, trending seasonal picks).
  - Contextual strategies consider the current context to suggest related items (for example, similarity, bought together, viewed together).

- Personalized strategies leverage individual customer data for tailored recommendations (for example, deep learning, collaborative filtering, affinity, recently viewed, last/recently purchased, bought with).

3. Define Hypotheses and KPIs

- Develop hypotheses: Use the following statement structure:
  - "IF we [proposed change] FOR [audience], THEN we will [impact on KPI] BECAUSE [reason behind the expected outcome]."
- Hypotheses are not facts: They are educated guesses based on data and knowledge.
- Set KPIs: Align with your business objectives and track the right metrics at each stage of the funnel (for example, click-through rate for the home page, add-to-cart for product pages).

4. Prioritize and Plan

- Prioritize tests: Consider both the impact (potential benefit) and effort (required resources) of each test.
- Use a prioritization matrix: This helps you visually assess and prioritize tests based on impact and effort.
- Create test briefs: Define the specifics of each test, including parameters, segmentation strategies, timeline, and duration.

5. Develop the Intended Experience

- Employ visual and technical expertise to create the customer experience based on the gathered information.

- Utilize a workflow to mock-up the final campaign, including copy, designs, and specifications.
- This stage can involve review and refinement before final approval.

6. Evaluate, Optimize, Repeat

- Personalization takes A/B testing further: It provides the best experience at an audience or individual level.
- Measure the impact of campaigns:
  - Determine the optimal test duration: Balance sample size with variation complexity to avoid false positives.
  - Analyze results: Consider metrics like "probability to be best" and uplift (performance differential between test and control).
  - Segment analysis: Measure how variations perform for different customer groups to refine targeting and personalization strategies.
- Turn insights into action:
  - Understand why winning variations performed well, and use this knowledge to inform future tests.
  - Continuously analyze data and refine personalization efforts over time.

TWO METHODOLOGIES FOR PERSONALIZATION

When combined with data analysis and testing, these methodologies can empower businesses to personalize experiences and achieve targeted improvements.

1. The Primary Audiences Approach

- Goal: Identify valuable customer segments and personalize experiences for individuals within each.

- Steps:
  - Define clear and impactful segmentation principles (for example, intent level, customer type).
  - Keep key audiences to a minimum (three to four) and mutually exclusive.
  - Ensure segments encompass most of your website traffic.
- Benefits:
  - Focused personalization for high-value segments.
  - Scalable and repeatable segmentation.
  - Aligns program road map and analysis with audience segments.

2. Evergreen Personalization Zones

- Goal: Establish dedicated areas on your website for constantly testing different content variations.
- Common zones: Home page banners, product listing page banners, navigation elements.
- Benefits:
  - Secure long-term access to test zones for consistent campaigns.
  - Facilitate testing different selling points and messages.
  - Gain insights into what resonates best with different audience segments.

PART TWO

YOUR
PERSONALIZATION
PLAYBOOK

The ever-expanding world of personalization can feel over-whelming, leaving even seasoned marketers unsure of their next step. Use this section as your Personalization Playbook; it offers an actionable plan packed with proven strategies and real-world examples from hundreds of successful campaigns across diverse industries.

For more than a decade, our team at Dynamic Yield has partnered with leading brands to implement innovative personalization across various channels, achieving significant uplifts in conversion rates, revenue per customer, average order value, and more. We've distilled our years of experience into actionable insights, revealing the core concepts behind each strategy.

By studying these successful campaigns and their underlying principles, you'll gain the confidence to launch your own personalized experiences, knowing you're building on a foundation of proven success.

We've categorized the personalization use cases into three core themes: (1) Personalized Discovery and Engagement, (2) Loyalty, Retention, and Recovery, and (3) Continuous Engagement and Optimization. This structure was carefully chosen to achieve several key objectives:

- **Simplicity:** We aimed to create a clear and concise framework that is easy to understand and navigate. The three themes represent distinct yet interconnected stages in the customer journey, providing a logical flow for exploring different personalization strategies.
- **Industry Agnosticism:** These themes are designed to be universally applicable across various industries and sectors. Regardless of your specific business domain, the core principles of discovery, engagement, loyalty, and optimization remain relevant and can be adapted to your unique context.
- **Customer-Centric Focus:** The framework prioritizes the customer experience at its core. Each theme emphasizes strategies catering to different aspects of the customer journey, aiming to build stronger relationships, drive engagement, and foster long-term success.

While this Personalization Playbook offers a comprehensive overview of various strategies, it's important to remember that there's no one-size-fits-all approach. We encourage you to explore the use cases through the lens of your unique business needs, available resources, and specific pain points.

Identify your biggest challenges related to customer engagement, conversion, or retention. If discovery is a major hurdle for your brand, prioritize use cases that enhance product or content discoverability. Conversely, if customer abandonment is a significant concern, focus on strategies that address this specific issue first.

Think of this playbook as a flexible road map that empowers you to tailor your personalization journey based on your unique context and goals. Dive into the sections that resonate most with your current priorities, and feel free to revisit different use cases as your needs evolve. Remember, continuous exploration and adaptation are key to unlocking the full potential of personalization for your brand.

PERSONALIZED DISCOVERY AND ENGAGEMENT

✖ ✦ ✖ ✳

This category encompasses use cases that personalize the customer journey, making it easier for customers to discover relevant products and information. By tailoring the experience to individual needs and preferences, these use cases improve discovery and enhance customer satisfaction, engagement, and conversion rates.

- **Guided Experiences:** Supports discovery by offering personalized guidance through complex processes or decisions, enhancing the ease with which customers can find products or information.
- **Recommendations:** Facilitates the discovery of new products, content, or services by suggesting options tailored to the customer's past interactions and stated interests.
- **Behavioral and Contextual-Based Personalization:** Enhances engagement by dynamically customizing the experience in response to customer behaviors or context (for example, location, device, time), making the interaction more responsive to immediate actions.

- **Personalized Navigation:** Improves the efficiency of discovery by adapting the navigation interface to the customer's behavior and preferences, making relevant content more accessible.

GUIDED EXPERIENCES

The What: Guided experiences focus on informing customers about which products, content, offers, or services best fit their needs, speeding up the product discovery process.

The concept of guided experiences revolves around providing personalized assistance to customers throughout their journey, fostering a sense of support and direction. The epitome of this approach lies in the traditional in-store experience. Upon entering a store, you're often greeted by salespeople who help you find what you need. This strategy translates seamlessly to the online world, where we can greet customers like virtual salespeople. This human-centric approach fosters customer engagement and ultimately leads to a more satisfying digital experience.

The Why: In an era where the human attention span is a scant eight seconds—less than that of a goldfish—how can brands capture and hold the interest of their potential customers? The digital marketplace is a crowded space. Websites have become templated and predictable, focusing more on showcasing an array of products rather than creating a unique, engaging, and personalized shopping experience.

Consider this: Low-intent audiences need more product education, medium-intent audiences need strong comparative information, while high-intent audiences need urgency and paired product recommendations. A generic, one-size-fits-all approach will fail to meet these unique needs. In response, consumers are increasingly seeking streamlined, tailored experiences to help them navigate this complexity.

Research shows that nearly half of consumers desire tools and services that save them the mental hassle of researching and picking items. Guided experiences can help brands break the mold and engender loyalty in customers who prefer a tailored shopping experience over a generic one.

The How: Here are three essential techniques to help brands make their guided experiences more effective.

1. Design a Clean, Thoughtful User Experience That Makes Discovery Easy

First and foremost, the user experience must be clean and intuitive. Customers should be able to navigate the site easily and find what they're looking for without feeling overwhelmed. This means designing a layout that is easy to understand, visually appealing, and clutter-free.

Incorporating elements like smart search functions, intuitive menus, and clear product categorization can make product and content discovery a breeze. Consider features such as filters that allow customers to narrow their search based on specific criteria or "predictive search" that offers relevant suggestions as customers type their queries.

A shift toward guided experiences would see pared-down home pages with less eclectic widgets or content, fewer featured products on product listing pages, and no more endless scroll pages. The focus would shift from quantity to quality, with less being more in terms of content.

2. Use Human-Sounding Copy with Transparent Messaging

Recommendation widgets are powerful tools, but they must be used correctly. The copy for these widgets should be transparent, purposeful, and informative, explaining clearly why a particular product is being recommended. Use human-sounding copy, and make sure your customer isn't guessing what a product does or what the brand stands for. This can help build trust and guide customers toward making a purchase. For example, instead of a generic "New products" message, you can write "New arrivals inspired by your recent searches" to provide more clarity and context.

Category headers, meanwhile, can be used to guide customers through the product selection process. By segmenting recommendation strategies and algorithm types according to the audience, brands can tailor the digital experience to meet the needs of different customer segments. This segment-focused approach can significantly enhance the experience, ensuring customers feel understood and valued on an emotional level.

3. Create Tools, Guides, Quizzes, and More

One of the core aspects of guided experiences is providing customers with the tools they need to make informed decisions. This can take many forms, from detailed product guides and tutorials that educate customers about the products or services to quizzes that help customers identify the offers that best meet their needs.

These tools should be interactive and engaging, turning the buying process from a mundane task into an enjoyable experience. They should also be easy to use and provide value, helping customers feel confident in their purchase decisions.

See It in Action

Interactive Quizzes and Product Displays

Interactive quizzes, personalized recommendations, and AI-powered conversational searches help customers find exactly what they're looking for, similar to how a salesperson might ask questions and suggest relevant items.

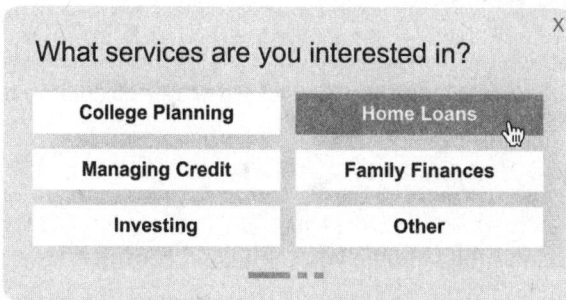

A mortgage lending company delivered hyperpersonalization to new customers almost immediately via guided experience surveys, asking them about their financial goals, retirement information, and more

The journey can continue with interactive product displays. Clicking on individual items reveals detailed information, purchase options, and personalized suggestions, akin to a salesperson showcasing different features and offering styling advice. Additionally, curated product combinations and product quizzes further assist in making informed decisions.

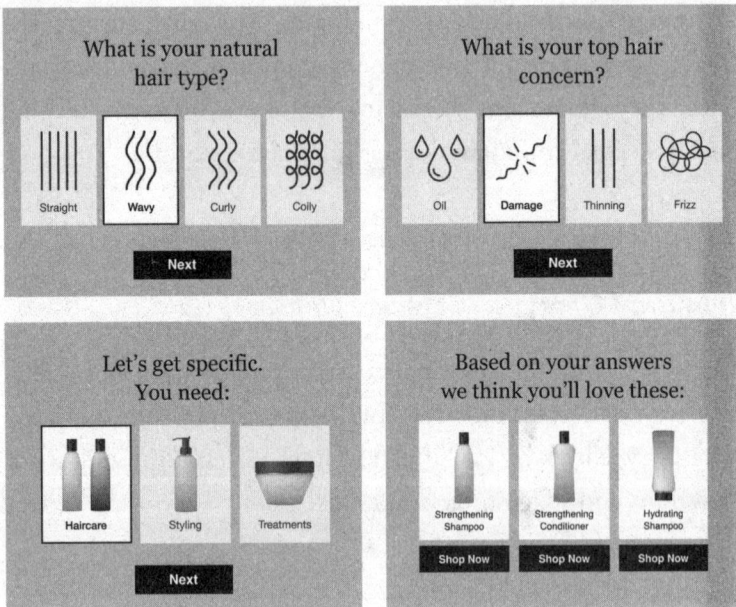

One beauty supplier provided quiz choices with descriptions that can make the fill-out process quick and smooth, helping with the paradox of choice

Comparison Tables

Comparison tables enable you to make recommendations based on the current product page so your customers can easily discover similar items. Empower your customers to make informed decisions and purchase the product that best fits their needs, reducing the risk of returns and exchanges.

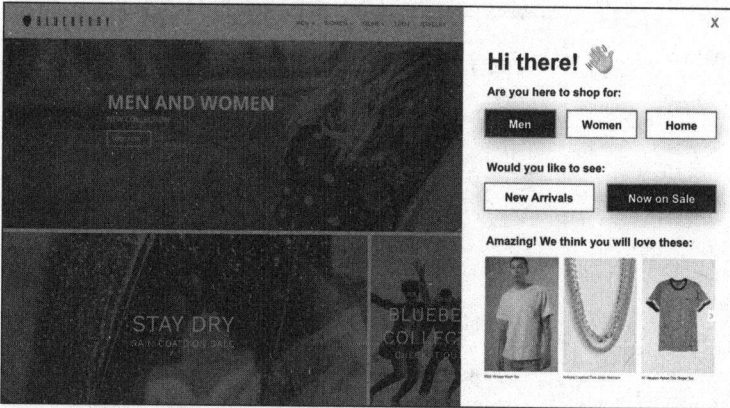

An example of chatbot-like recommendations that mimic an in-store assistant experience, driving self-segmentation and helping customers find the most relevant items faster

A jeweler added a product comparison table to its product detail pages, allowing visitors to compare and contrast similar items

Post-Purchase Survey

Guided experiences aren't limited to the product discovery phase and can be implemented across the customer journey. By implementing these diverse applications of guided experiences, you can create a more engaging and personalized online experience, ultimately leading to increased customer satisfaction and conversion rates.

HOW DID YOU HEAR ABOUT US?

- Social Media
- Advertisement
- Podcast Advertisement
- Search
- Local Event
- Article
- Word of Mouth
- Other

SUBMIT >

A retailer surveys first-time purchasers on what attracted them to
the site upon mouse exit behavior, using answers to further personalize
as well as create look-alike audiences

RECOMMENDATIONS

The What: Different customers at different stages of the journey have different needs, and identifying the right opportunities to algorithmically match the most appropriate products, offers, or content to each individual customer can amplify their experience, push them to purchase, and increase their total purchase value. This is why recommendation engines exist.

High-impact recommendations that resonate with your customers and drive them to convert rely on several critical factors: selecting the optimal recommendation strategy, defining the context of the web page or app screen it is running on, and taking into account the characteristics, preferences, and attributes of the customer.

Recommendation strategies provide the logic behind the item selection for your product or content recommendations. These strategies determine the decisioning logic behind which products, content, or offers to display. These experiences are built to meet consumers' needs and demands, as well as drive engagement and revenue to boost brands' bottom lines.

Today, the ability to effectively deploy recommendations is a critical necessity for companies that manage extensive inventories of products or content.

Product Recommendations

A product recommendation is a suggestion for an item someone might be interested in purchasing. These suggestions are often based on data and can come from various sources, including customers' past behavior, similar customer profiles, and product attributes. E-commerce brands and other online platforms commonly use product recommendations to help customers discover new products, increase sales, and personalize the shopping experience.

Content Recommendations

A content recommendation is a suggestion for a piece of content, such as an article or video, that someone might be interested in consuming. Similar to product recommendations, these suggestions are often based on data and can come from various sources, including visitors' interests, preferences, and behavior. Companies can use content recommendations to ensure customers are exposed only to content they are interested in, increasing the likelihood of engagement.

The Why: Evidence of the monumental impact of recommendations is seen across industry giants.

- Amazon leverages its recommendation engine to account for a staggering 35 percent of its total sales, demonstrating the compelling influence of personalized suggestions on consumer purchasing decisions.
- Netflix, another behemoth in the entertainment sector, attributes an impressive 80 percent of its viewer activity to its recommendation system, underscoring the critical role of personalized content in maintaining viewer engagement and reducing churn.
- Similarly, Spotify's success with features like Discover Weekly highlights the power of personalization in music streaming, enhancing customer satisfaction and fostering a stronger emotional connection with the platform.

These examples underscore the transformative potential of recommendation systems, not just as tools for navigation but as strategic assets that drive engagement, revenue, and sustained competitive advantage.

The How: Effective recommendation engines tailor their approach to each customer by leveraging available data, context, behavioral activity, and other factors to encourage engagement and action. For instance, new customers with limited data might see general "Most Popular" suggestions, while those with a history of interactions are presented with more contextually relevant recommendations. The most personalized experiences are reserved for repeat customers, who benefit from "Recommended for You" widgets and other tailored suggestions throughout their online journey, reflecting the sophistication of modern recommendation systems in understanding and catering to individual customer preferences.

As customer loyalty intensifies, so do expectations for personalized interactions. The depth of a customer's engagement with a brand directly correlates with the richness of data available to tailor recommendations, creating a virtuous cycle where increased data points lead to more personalized experiences. Recognizing the value in these customized interactions, customers are more inclined to stay logged into their accounts across devices. This loyalty is rewarded with recommendations that not only reflect their past browsing and purchasing habits but are also finely tuned to their preferences for specific brands, product lines, colors, price ranges, and even shipping options.

Setting Up Audience-Centered Merchandising Rules

Although automated algorithms have a strong track record, your merchandizers have tremendous expertise and insight into your customers. A flexible recommendation engine allows you to support manual merchandising rules, such as pinning a specific item or including/excluding a particular set of items from the automated recommendation results. For example, merchandizers can set rules that inform the product recommendations engine to:

- include popular items in a product category a consumer has viewed over a set period of time (for example, displaying a popular item in "men's shorts" to a visitor who has viewed at least two pairs of men's shorts in the past thirty days);
- recommend highly profitable items to consumers who have purchased or added to their carts items valued at two hundred dollars or more in the past seven days;

- refrain from displaying clearance items promoted in other areas of the brand's site to high-value customers; and
- create more granular rules to accomplish specific business goals, such as moving remnant stock or slow-moving inventory.

Additionally, merchandising rules can be combined with personalization to hypertarget certain audience segments. Demographic, geographic, and behavioral data are all high-value data points that should be leveraged in product recommendations. With data available on every customer, create merchandising rules that will help better tailor their site experiences. For example, if the weather is cold in Boston, you can create rules that automatically recommend winter apparel to Bostonians. Additionally, depending on the available data, the system can create more granular recommendations according to other identifiers, such as gender, household income, brand affinities, and more.

Enhancing the recommendation engine with custom business logic can significantly improve its performance in certain scenarios. This involves integrating your proprietary formulas, product combinations, or "lookbooks" into the recommendation engine, enabling the customization of algorithms and decisioning logic. Such an approach opens many possibilities, including creating immersive "Shop the Look" experiences and combining in-house expertise with the engine's AI capabilities.

Optimizing Recommendations

Recommendations offer two great routes for optimization: A/B testing both the widget UX and algorithms.

Experimenting and Testing New Layouts

Recommendations aren't always made in a rotating carousel laid out in one row. In fact, there is no single best template, and optimizing the look and feel of your recommendations can make a world of difference—especially on mobile web and native apps.

Marketers need the flexibility to alter, change, and customize the layout and functionality of every widget. A flexible recommendation engine will allow you to incorporate tests and personalization tactics that position recommendations in different areas of the page and site for different audiences and allow you to alter the layout or recommendations according to every visitor type.

Experimenting and Testing Recommendation Campaigns

A/B testing different recommendation strategies will come in handy when looking to understand which recommendation strategy is working best. It will allow you to refine and increase the impact of every campaign in real time and identify key insights and learnings for the long term. And incorporating different merchandising rules for product recommendations will further enhance your experimentation capabilities, allowing you to identify key opportunities for revenue generation. Be sure to harness customer data to effectively segment audiences and build new experiences that will suit consumers and reach them where they are, ensuring they are always recommended products they've expressed interest in or are likely interested in. Remember: The more personalized the site experience, the more likely a consumer is to convert (and return).

Recommendations as a Key Revenue Driver

Recommendation strategies vary greatly from one another, and experimenting with strategies will help improve revenue and create richer experiences. By remaining nimble, testing different placements, and analyzing performance data, you'll refine your overall strategy to better tailor the site experience for every customer. And once you're comfortable, play with advanced settings, segmentation strategies, and merchandising rules to extract the highest value from every audience segment to start realizing your highest ROI.

See It in Action

On-Page Product Recommendations

Product recommendations are crucial across various stages of the digital customer journey, from a brand's home page, product listing, and category pages to product detail pages and cart pages,

RECOMMENDED FOR YOU

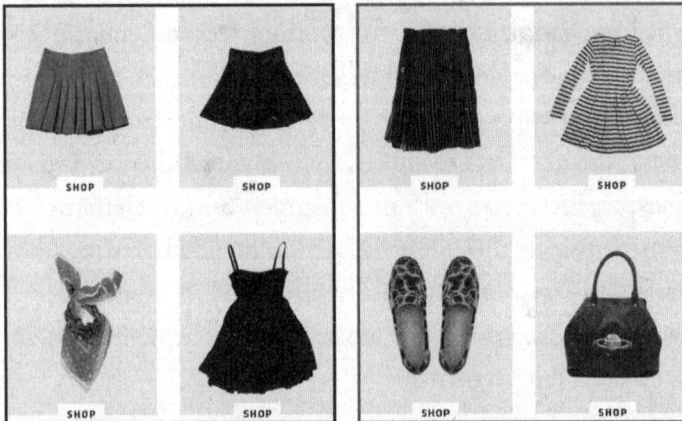

A recommendation widget with a hybrid strategy rendered on a product detail page to display "Similar" and "Bought Together" products

often enhanced by overlays and recommendation widgets. These recommendations can also extend beyond traditional web properties into newsletters, digital receipts, native mobile apps, and even physical retail environments. This expansive reach allows for a unified and personalized experience across all channels.

Side-Door Traffic-Targeted Recommendations

Referral and search traffic that arrive directly on a specific category or product page often provide a fleeting opportunity to engage a site visitor. And more times than not, brands miss their chance to capture a customer's attention, resulting in a page bounce. To avoid this, marketers need to entice customers to stay

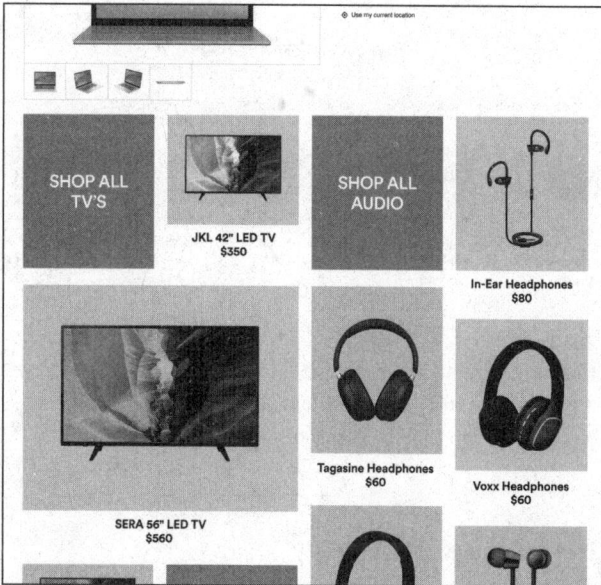

An electronics retailer uses a Pinterest-like recommendation widget below the main featured product on the PDP, encouraging deeper browsing without having to leave the page

onsite longer by surfacing similar products to the one in view. To do so, expose this traffic—known as side-door traffic—to various relevant, captivating products.

Sales-Driven Recommendations

Everyone is interested in reduced-price items, including your most loyal shoppers, who are happy to inflate their cart with additional sale items together with the full-priced items they've selected. Since sale items are relevant to everyone, they should be recommended anywhere on the site. Contrary to some schools of thought, there is no reason to restrict sale items only to the Sale and Outlet sections of the site. Doing so can significantly limit your average order value and conversion rate.

Top Savings For You
Most Popular

Charcoal Grill	Electric Oven	Window AC Unit	Chrome Faucet	Drip Coffee Maker
★★★★⯨	★★★★⯨	★★★★★	★★★★★	★★★★⯨
$34.99	$399.99	$199.99	$79.99	$24.99

An electronics store opted to personalize a product recommendations widget on the home page for returning shoppers, featuring on-sale items that fit a customer's affinity profile

Live Streaming Recommendations

As the use of recommendation widgets increases, they've been popping up across channels in inventive ways. For example,

Example of personalized product discovery during live stream shopping, whereby video watchers can receive recommendations based on what appears in the live stream as well as their behavior

live stream retail on channels such as YouTube, Facebook, and Instagram has seen massive popularity and adoption in recent years. But these live streams often include links only to the set number of products highlighted in the video. Brands can provide an even more differentiated component to these interactive experiences by adding multiple layers of personalized, AI-driven recommendations that ensure individual shoppers see products according to their unique affinity, historical purchases, and other important buying intent signals.

Email Recommendations

Email still remains one of the strongest channels for driving engagement and revenue, and it's ripe for optimization opportunities executed through personalization.

A retailer ensures relevant products in every email blast with a personalized algorithm combined with filters matching its theme (like recommending sunglasses by affinity) so each customer receives items fitting their own style and preferences

Affinity-Based Emails

By showing potential customers the products most relevant to them, you can increase conversion rates and revenue from email.

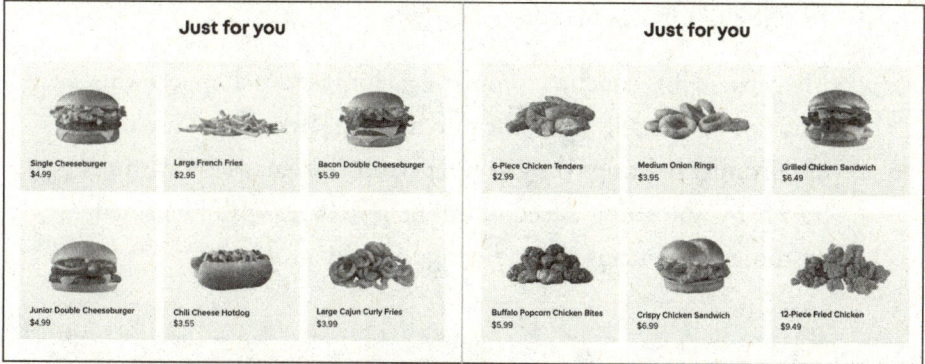

Just for you			Just for you		
Single Cheeseburger $4.99	Large French Fries $2.95	Bacon Double Cheeseburger $5.99	6-Piece Chicken Tenders $2.99	Medium Onion Rings $3.95	Grilled Chicken Sandwich $6.49
Junior Double Cheeseburger $4.99	Chili Cheese Hotdog $3.55	Large Cajun Curly Fries $3.99	Buffalo Popcorn Chicken Bites $5.99	Crispy Chicken Sandwich $6.99	12-Piece Fried Chicken $9.49

A leading global QSR created and tailored content for two different audiences: one with an affinity for chicken and one with an affinity for beef via a simple code snippet embedded into its ESP

Intent-Based Email Recommendations

Apart from affinity, intent is also a great strategy to use for personalized email recommendations.

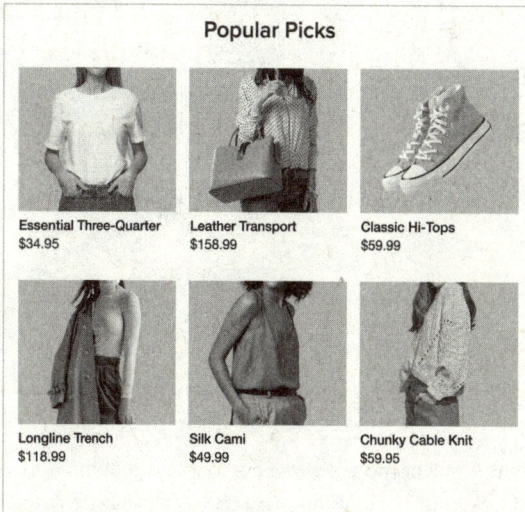

Popular Picks		
Essential Three-Quarter $34.95	Leather Transport $158.99	Classic Hi-Tops $59.99
Longline Trench $118.99	Silk Cami $49.99	Chunky Cable Knit $59.95

A fashion retailer reduced email development times by dynamically personalizing different content blocks within the same email according to audiences of different intent levels, which also drove more purchases from each

In-Store to Online Recommendations

Many email lists contain customer data for in-store shoppers who may not have made an online purchase yet. Brands can use this opportunity to bridge the gap and personalize emails for in-store buyers by uploading a feed of offline purchases with identified customers to generate an individual affinity profile.

A retailer serves email campaigns with content and recommendations (right) personalized based on their offline purchasers' affinities (left), increasing the conversion of in-store to online purchases

TRANSMISSION FROM YOUR PERSONALIZED FUTURE:

BOOST CONFIDENCE WITH EMAILS TO

ENCOURAGE RETURN VISITS

Email marketing and newsletters have one purpose—to bring traffic back to the website. Therefore, content and detailed specifications that cause the recipient to think and calculate before they return to a site should be avoided. Price, especially when high, will often scare off and deter an email recipient. High-resolution images as well as high-ranking and favorable reviews will grab attention, eventually drawing a customer back to the site.

Content Versus Product Recommendations

For some stages of the customer journey, content recommendations will work better than product recommendations to

A consumer financial services company adjusts its recommendations according to different customer journey stages, evolving as individuals return, become card members, and so forth. Returning customers are served content recommendations (left) whereas new customers see product recommendations (right) effectively educate site visitors on the resources available to them. Then, as the customer–brand relationship advances, product recommendations become more salient.

Content Discovery

Using personalized content recommendations based on visitors' interests, preferences, and behavior, companies can be sure customers are exposed only to content they are interested in, increasing the likelihood of engagement, decreasing exit rates, and increasing site loyalty.

How to save more this year

To save more money, follow these essential tips
Read now >

What you need to know about home equity
Watch video >

Foods of the future: 5 trends to watch for in 2020
Read now >

Car buying trends you need to know for 2020
Read now >

See more >

A financial organization personalizes bundles of offers and content based on affinity, spending power, and preferences, with merchandising rules used to showcase articles meant to upsell or highlight different categories across slots

BEHAVIOR AND CONTEXT-BASED PERSONALIZATION

The What:

Behavior-Based Personalization

Behavior-based personalization is rooted in the understanding that an individual's actions paint a far more accurate picture of their preferences and needs than demographic stereotypes alone ever could. Whether it's the articles a customer reads, the products they browse, or the music they stream, each action is a breadcrumb leading to a deeper understanding of their true interests and inclinations. By prioritizing behavior over demographics, or combining the two dimensions, brands can craft highly relevant, engaging experiences that resonate on a personal level, fostering a sense of individuality and connection. Here are some examples of behavior-based personalization:

- **Past purchases:** An e-commerce platform utilizes a customer's past purchases to recommend similar or complementary products.
- **Search behavior:** A travel booking website tracks the destinations and types of accommodations a customer searches for to offer personalized vacation recommendations.
- **Browsing behavior:** A news website dynamically adjusts the articles displayed on its home page for each customer based on the types of articles they spend the most time reading.
- **Email interaction:** A financial service brand changes the content of its marketing emails based on how a customer interacts with previous emails, sending more targeted promotions or information.

Context-Based Personalization

Context-based personalization, on the other hand, goes beyond behavior and offers a dynamic and relevant experience by considering the immediate situation and specific customer needs. Contextual personalization leverages other real-time factors like the customer's location, device, time of day, weather conditions, referral data, and more. Here are some examples of contextual-based personalization:

- **Event-based personalization:** A fitness app might recommend specific workout routines based on the customer's proximity to a gym or upcoming participation in a race.
- **Device-based personalization:** A telco commerce website offering mobile devices might adjust its product recommendations based on whether the customer is browsing on a phone, tablet, or desktop, considering the device type and operating system being used.
- **Referral data:** A financial services website might suggest specific credit cards based on referral data from affiliated sites.
- **Language preference:** A website or app might automatically switch its language interface based on the customer's location or browsing history, providing a more comfortable experience.

Behavior and context can be used to tailor promotions and content across email campaigns, digital display ads, mobile push notifications, and almost any other means of digital communication.

The How: In behavior and context-based personalization, the process of understanding customer motivations unfolds in two clear steps.

Step One: Observe Behavior and Monitor Context

Track and analyze customer interactions, such as what content they read, which products they view, how often they view these products, and the duration of their engagement. This data collection is crucial for identifying patterns that reveal customer interests and behaviors.

Step Two: Extrapolate Intent

Use the observed behavioral and contextual data to segment customers into affinity-based audiences. For each audience, develop targeted experiences with messaging and recommendations tailored to their specific interests. This strategy ensures that personalization efforts are grounded in actual customer behavior, leading to more relevant and effective engagements.

See It in Action

Personalized Home Page Banners

The home page is typically the initial point of discovery for many customers; therefore, the experience shouldn't be static—home page banners should, instead, be utilized as an essential first touchpoint. By replacing generic home page banners with content personalized to the customer, brands can encourage all types of engagement, such as clicks and site searches, that will ultimately reduce bounce rate and potentially increase revenue, conversions, and other important KPIs. Update banners based on whatever data is available, using contextual data such as visitor type, traffic source, location, or behavior-based data like browsing and purchase history, or real-time browsing signals.

A booking portal leverages past customer behavior and demographics to expose banners proven to increase engagement among key segments: resort lovers, families with kids (below), budget travelers (top), cruise lovers, etc.

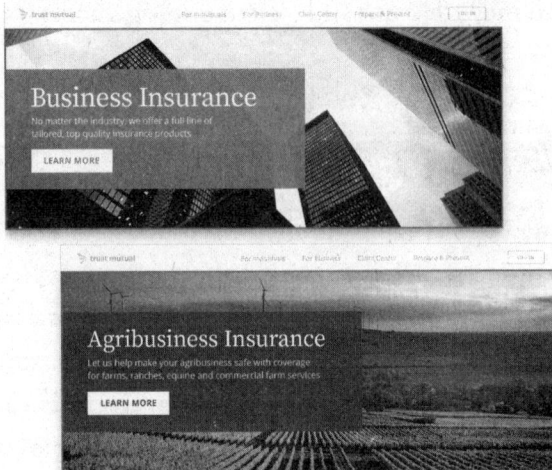

A consumer insurance company uses contextual data such as weather and location to deploy welcome messages, email sign-up overlays, and more to personalize the home page for first-time, anonymous visitors in real time. Customers from NYC see messages for business insurance (top), whereas people in Nebraska are served messages for agriculture insurance (bottom)

Personalized Notifications

Not willing to give up that much real estate? There are many smaller ways to add contextual personalization across channels using notifications and pop-ups.

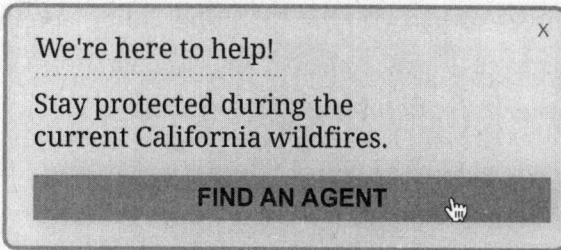

We're here to help!

Stay protected during the current California wildfires.

FIND AN AGENT

An insurance company uses geo-based notifications to highlight relevant insurance plans and encourage proactive customer action ahead of scenarios like natural disasters

Location-Based Offers

Contextual personalization can also help you grow your local business. Free shipping has become a significant factor in a shopper's decision to complete a purchase. And while it can be costly for brands to assume these delivery costs, marketers can balance promotional offers with lower shipping thresholds for visitors in the area.

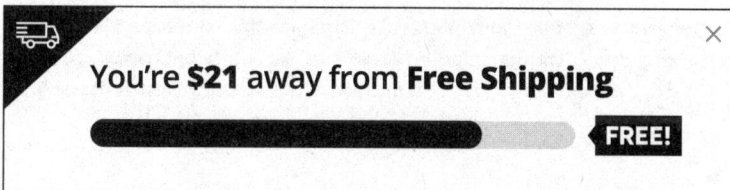

You're **$21** away from **Free Shipping**

FREE!

A wholesale retailer uses geotargeting to offer free shipping promotions to customers located near their shipping center

Weather-Aware Recommendations

Weather targeting is empowering organizations to anticipate patterns of demand and tap into the moods, needs, and purchase intentions of their customers. Weather targeting is the practice of tailoring influential messages to visitors based on local temperatures or weather conditions and is accomplished by integrating a real-time weather forecast data stream into your existing personalization platform.

A sports retailer greets anonymous visitors with weather-appropriate products. For a sunny day in London, recommendations like T-shirts and polos are given (above), while a rainy day in Finland spurs jackets and hoodies (below)

Another retailer set up banners for every type of weather condition to optimize product discovery, with multiple variations per each weather condition all continuously optimized year-round—see one variation for rainy conditions (above) and another for snow (below)

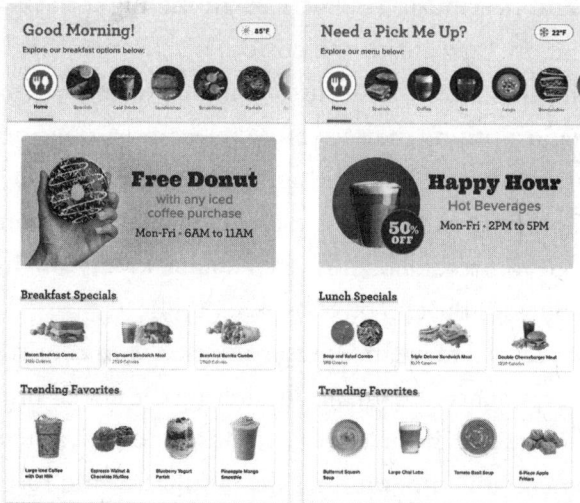

A restaurant utilizes location data to suggest more relevant drive-thru and kiosk experiences to anonymous customers based on the time of day and weather conditions: A breakfast menu on a sunny day in California (left) recommends different options than lunch on a chilly day in Minnesota (right)

PERSONALIZED NAVIGATION

The What: Personalized navigation represents an interesting approach to how websites and apps interact with their users, tailoring the user interface and navigation elements to meet individual preferences and needs. This customization leverages data analytics and customer behavior patterns to rearrange menus, suggest content, and highlight features that align with a customer's interests and past interactions.

For example, consider an online retail platform that dynamically adjusts its menu to display categories or products a customer frequently browses. This not only enhances the shopping experience by making it more intuitive and less time-consuming but also increases the likelihood of discovery and purchase of products perfectly suited to the customer's tastes.

Similarly, a bank's app might analyze a customer's transaction history and previously read articles to highlight navigational items that are relevant to the customer's profile. This level of personalization ensures that customers are presented with information and options that are most relevant to their financial habits and goals, making the app more useful and engaging. Such tailored experiences foster a strong emotional connection between customers and brands, encouraging loyalty and frequent interaction with the app or website.

But it's crucial to balance personalization with consistency in the user experience. Dramatically altering the layout or navigation structure of a site or app can confuse or disorient returning users, potentially undermining the familiarity and ease of use that keeps them coming back. While personalization can significantly enhance the user experience, it should be implemented thoughtfully to avoid disrupting the core navigational framework. Adjustments should be subtle and focused on augmenting the navigation process, such as fine-tuning menu items based on gender for fashion sites or affinity toward specific brands or product categories. This approach ensures that while users benefit from a more personalized and efficient browsing experience, they also enjoy a consistent and recognizable interface each time they visit.

The Why: When shoppers don't know what they want quite yet, they turn to a brand's navigation to begin their journey. But this can quickly result in frustration, as the process of clicking through category pages and layering in filters can be time-consuming. Instead of forcing the customer to start this work from scratch, brands can personalize some of the navigation elements to surface filters according to customers' unique affinities. Doing so will decrease both the time it takes for the shopper to find products of interest and the time to purchase.

The How: Enhancing your personalized navigation strategy involves several best practices that can significantly improve the user experience on your website or app. Here are a couple of key recommendations to consider.

Incorporate Personalized Product Recommendations

Utilize the space within your navigation menus effectively by integrating personalized product recommendations. When a user expands the navigation menu, display items specifically tailored to their interests and past behavior. This maximizes the use of your site's real estate and increases the chances of discovery and purchase, providing a more customized shopping experience.

Embrace A/B Testing for Navigation Optimization

There is no one-size-fits-all solution for designing the perfect site navigation, particularly in the dynamic e-commerce sector. Customer demographics can vary widely, each with its own set of preferences and expectations. To navigate this diversity, it's crucial to adopt a testing mindset. Experiment with different aspects of your navigation, including the placement and design of menus, the arrangement of product categories in either tiered or fixed menus, and the personalization of filter menu items based on individual browsing histories. Testing different messaging variations is also essential. Each test should uncover what resonates best with your audience segments.

See It in Action

Affinity-Driven Navigation

The order in which you present menu items is also a way to optimize your site navigation. While you may have a default order you present to the average visitor or new customer, using

MOST LOVED CATEGORIES

SHOES   BAGS   JEWELRY   WATCHES   SUNGLASSES   HATS

An apparel retailer uses a customer affinity strategy to surface the most relevant and personalized filters for each site visitor as a means of category navigation optimization

An electronics retailer personalized the order of its side navigation menu based on every visitor's preferences (control on left, variation on right for those most interested in purchasing TVs)

affinity data, you can tailor the order of menu items to personalize the experience on a more individual basis based on a customer's preferences. Not only will it expedite the discovery process, but it can also drive conversions more efficiently.

Personalized Navigation for Side-Door Traffic

Although the home page typically used to be the initial point of entry to websites, more and more visitors are now landing on product pages, whether they come from social networks, organic search, email campaigns, or ads. Because of this, brands are seeking to improve continual discovery by enabling visitors to easily navigate back to a product's main category page. This is particularly important for incoming traffic from paid search and product listing campaigns, where there is a direct investment in bringing visitors to your site.

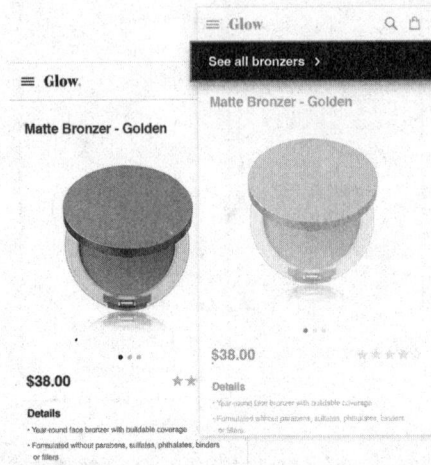

An online beauty merchant personalized the navigation header to promote the item's category for visitors who land directly on product detail pages (control on the left, variation on the right), improving discovery and reducing bounce rate from search traffic

LOYALTY, RETENTION, AND RECOVERY

✕ ✛ ✖ ✳

This category focuses on use cases that aim to build stronger relationships with customers, encourage continued engagement, and win back those who might be disengaging. By fostering loyalty and addressing potential churn, these use cases contribute to long-term customer value and brand advocacy.

- **Loyalty-Driven Personalization:** Deepens loyalty and encourages retention by offering rewards or experiences that recognize and cater to a customer's history and loyalty status.
- **Postpurchase Messages:** Strengthens the relationship with customers by sending tailored communications after a purchase, encouraging continued engagement and loyalty.
- **Time-Based Abandonment Messages:** Targets customers who have abandoned their carts or browsing sessions with timed reminders, encouraging them to complete their intended actions.
- **Exit-Intent Messages:** Captures the attention of customers who are about to leave the site with targeted

messages or offers, aiming to decrease abandonment rates.

- **Push Notifications:** Maintains engagement through tailored notifications, keeping customers informed and interested even when they're not actively using the service.
- **Back-to-Context Reminders:** Encourages customers to return by reminding them of their last interaction point, reducing barriers to reengagement.

LOYALTY-DRIVEN PERSONALIZATION

The What: Successful loyalty programs hinge on a compelling value proposition, a personalized customer experience, and a streamlined registration process. A robust value proposition considers diverse reward systems, not limited to monetary transactions. Engaging customers through nontransactional behaviors like app engagement or purchase frequency can set a program apart. Rewards can range from traditional point systems to innovative surprise and delight tactics, fostering emotional loyalty. Once defined, this value proposition must be brought to life across all platforms.

The Why: Amid the cacophony of digital noise and fierce competition, consumers gravitate toward brands that offer relevant, engaging, and convenient experiences across various channels. This paradigm shift not only bolsters brand retention and revenue potential but also caters efficiently to consumer desires. At the heart of this transformation is a balance between data privacy protection and a human-centric approach. Personalization heralds a new epoch of consumer focus, reshaping engagement dynamics for the better. Winning brands in this era excel in contextual understanding, perception management, and expectation fulfillment, offering smart recommendations and forging authentic connections with their customers. Interestingly, the true measure of success in this realm isn't revenue or ROI but rather customer loyalty.

Reflect on your customers' expectations from interactions with your brand. They seek *value*, *utility*, and *enjoyment*. Personalization, a confluence of automation, AI, and human oversight, centralizes these three dimensions, offering scalable, extraordinary experiences. Customers' needs are the bedrock of their relationship with a brand. Meeting these needs shapes their expectations and subsequent behaviors. Emotional needs also play a pivotal role, with many customers seeking an emotional bond and a sense of care from the brands they patronize. Preferences, dictated by individual expectations, guide how brands should deliver their products and services. Empathy emerges as a key driver in this intricate web of needs, wants, and preferences, forging sustainable trust, loyalty, and advocacy.

Your customers desire experiences that are:

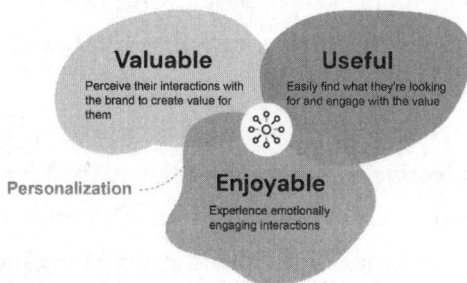

Valuable
Perceive their interactions with the brand to create value for them

Useful
Easily find what they're looking for and engage with the value

Personalization

Enjoyable
Experience emotionally engaging interactions

- **Value** is a clear factor; customers want to feel that the time and energy they invest in interacting with a brand benefits them. This value can be tangible, such as a product or service that meets their needs, or intangible, such as gaining helpful information or having a positive experience.

- **Efficiency** is another crucial factor. In today's fast-paced world, customers appreciate interactions that allow them to quickly and effortlessly discover what they seek. This could be facilitated through intuitive website design, efficient customer service, or streamlined purchasing processes.
- **Enjoyment**, although subjective, is also a fundamental part of the equation. This is evident in the fact that customers often compare their experiences with various brands to those they have with entertainment platforms like TikTok, Netflix, and Spotify. They desire not just a transaction but an engaging and enjoyable experience.

Loyalty programs, driven by personalization, are no longer just transactional benefits but emotional engagements. Research indicates that 74 percent of buyers join loyalty programs for personalized experiences and exclusive offers. Customers engaged in such programs are more likely to promote the brand. Conversely, a lack of value, effort-intensive reward systems, and irrelevant offers can drive customers away.

The How: Segmenting audiences according to their loyalty status helps brands better nurture relationships with their most valuable customers. For these individuals, experiences should look significantly different from what a first-time or even returning visitor might receive. Brands should therefore leverage all available data on current loyalty members and use it to segment audiences, serving highly targeted messaging and promotions that not only confirm their special membership treatment but also inspire further activity.

Personalization enhances loyalty, creating a cycle where increased loyalty fuels the need for more personalization. The more loyal you become as a customer, the higher the expectation you have for personalization. Effective loyalty programs can quickly become instrumental in gathering insights, capturing digital spending, differentiating brands, and strengthening customer relationships.

See It in Action

Loyalty-Based Communication

Tailoring messages, promotions, and experiences to loyalty status can make each interaction unique.

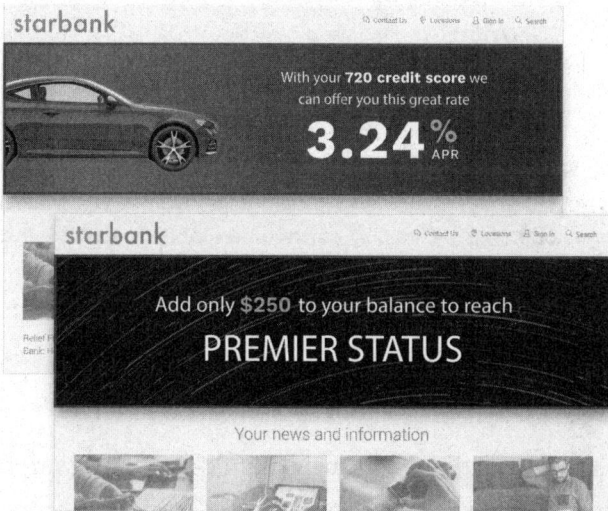

A bank leverages data regarding customer attributes like lifetime value and spending capacity to personalize the home page, showcasing exclusive offers based on credit score (above) and loyalty status (below)

hello gorgeous!

YOU'RE ONLY $150 AWAY FROM KEEPING YOUR GOLD BEAUTY PASS STATUS & LOYALTY PERKS.

A beauty brand serves individualized communication using loyalty status via a notification banner to boost engagement and increase average order value

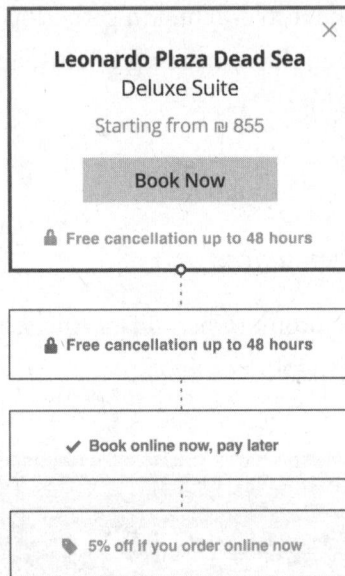

Leonardo Plaza Dead Sea
Deluxe Suite

Starting from ₪ 855

Book Now

🔒 Free cancellation up to 48 hours

🔒 Free cancellation up to 48 hours

✔ Book online now, pay later

🏷 5% off if you order online now

A hotel chain identifies customers by their hotel loyalty club affiliation and encourages bookings by adding personalized incentives below the main CTA button

Loyalty-Based Emails

You can personalize emails using dynamic content variations and serve customers experiences populated with their loyalty data. This can generate thousands of different email experiences with a single send, minimizing the lift for the company and creating a stronger relationship with each individual. Ultimately, this strategy drives more awareness and use of a loyalty program, increasing recurring revenue per customer over time.

Hey Sarah, let's use your points!

You have 735 points for your next purchase.

Redeem Now

Use your point towards these items

Vintage Crew Neck
499 points

Charlie 5 Series
175 points

Coastal Crew Neck
698 points

Everet Wash Shorts
714 points

A retailer dynamically tailors images embedded in its email to contain an individual's name and current loyalty points, with a recommendation widget displaying only products that fall within their loyalty tier

Gamification

Gamification has proven to drive higher rates of engagement than traditional experiences—an exciting opportunity for brands to nurture relationships with customers in a more immersive way. For example, gamifying a loyalty program can drive members from one tier to the next through personalized recommendations, targeted content for each customer, and tailored rewards, resulting in the purchase of more products and rewards earned.

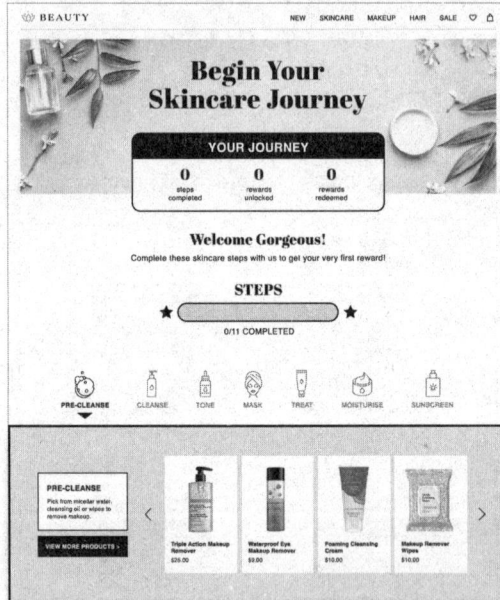

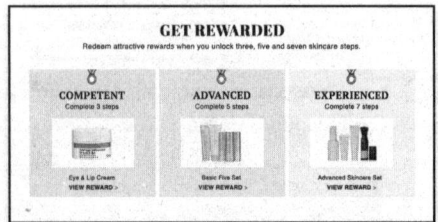

A beauty brand orchestrates an end-to-end gamified journey, driving customers from one loyalty tier to the next through additional spending with dynamic content widgets, messaging, and recommendations across web and mobile app

In-Store Loyalty

Loyalty can extend its influence in-store as well, with personalized kiosks and digital boards (as well as on the mobile app). By making loyalty information prominent, you can (1) promote the loyalty program and remind customers of the rewards associated with repeat business; (2) increase product discovery by highlighting new products available to try "for free" with points; and (3) get customers thinking about items they'd like to have, increasing the chance that a customer would overspend their point count and generate additional revenue with a larger cart size. Overall,

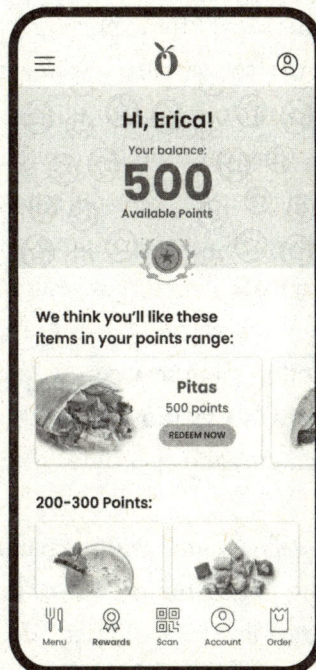

Restaurants are leveraging customer login data (loyalty points and purchase history) to enhance the dining experience with personalized offers and recommendations

this strategy leads to a lift in revenue from returning customers and increased engagement with the loyalty program.

POSTPURCHASE MESSAGES

The What: In today's competitive market, where customer acquisition costs are consistently on the rise across various industries, the significance of nurturing existing customer relationships cannot be overstated. The emphasis on loyalty, retention, and recovery strategies is paramount for businesses aiming to sustain and grow their market presence. Postpurchase messages play a critical role in this dynamic, serving as a bridge to transform onetime transactions into ongoing dialogues.

Existing customers are often more receptive and offer a higher potential for sales compared to new prospects. This is because a foundation of trust and familiarity has already been established. Recognizing this opportunity, brands are encouraged to develop a comprehensive postpurchase communication strategy. Such a strategy should focus not only on thanking the customer but also on adding value through relevant content, offering personalized recommendations, and soliciting feedback to improve products and services. By doing so, businesses can enhance customer satisfaction, stimulate repeat purchases, foster brand engagement, and encourage the spread of positive word-of-mouth.

The benefits of a well-executed postpurchase strategy are multifaceted, contributing to a virtuous cycle of increased customer loyalty, higher lifetime value, and, ultimately, augmented revenue streams. This approach is applicable across sectors, from retail and e-commerce to services and technology, highlighting its universal relevance and potential for impact.

The Why: In the context of e-commerce, the utility of post-purchase strategies extends beyond mere order confirmation. These communications serve as strategic tools to further engage customers in a nonintrusive and personalized manner. But the principles underlying the effective use of tailored postpurchase messages are applicable across a broad spectrum of industries. For instance, in the service sector, a follow-up message after a service appointment can reinforce the customer's decision, offer maintenance tips, or introduce complementary services. In the technology industry, messages can educate customers about product features, upcoming updates, or exclusive offers for accessories and expansions.

The postpurchase period is a critical juncture for new customers, especially those acquired through referrals. It represents their first direct interaction with the brand beyond the initial transaction. Leveraging this touchpoint effectively can solidify the customer's perception of the brand, turning an initial purchase into the start of a long-term relationship. By maximizing the value delivered through these communications, businesses can significantly increase the likelihood of repeat business, elevate the average number of recurring orders per customer, and enhance overall customer lifetime value.

Tailored and timely postpurchase messages offer a unique opportunity to build lasting customer relationships, differentiate from competitors, and drive sustainable growth. By understanding and leveraging the nuances of these communications, businesses can unlock their full potential to foster loyalty, enhance retention, and facilitate recovery.

The How: Postpurchase messages are a golden opportunity to enhance customer experience, reinforce brand loyalty, and stimulate repeat business. To truly capitalize on this opportunity, it's essential to adopt a strategic approach that resonates with your customer base and aligns with your brand values. Here are some best practices to guide you in optimizing your postpurchase communication strategy.

Offer Promotions

A common tactic employed by many businesses, especially in the retail sector, is to include exclusive offers or discounts in postpurchase messages. This strategy can effectively incentivize first-time buyers to become repeat customers. The key, however, is to balance the attractiveness of the offer with the sustainability of your business model. While significant discounts can drive immediate sales, they should be employed judiciously to avoid undermining the perceived value of your products or services and to ensure they do not negatively impact your overall sales performance.

Go Beyond the "Hard Sell"

Effective postpurchase messaging strategies extend beyond mere attempts to secure the next sale. They should aim to cultivate a deeper relationship with the customer by providing value beyond the transaction. This approach can take many forms, depending on your industry and the nature of your products or services.

For example, fashion retailers can personalize follow-up emails with curated looks and product recommendations that incorporate the purchased item. Including customer-generated content or social proof can also enhance the perceived value of your brand and products.

See It in Action

Shipment Confirmations with Product Recommendations

With proper customer consent, you can maximize the impact of shipping confirmation emails by adding a product recommendation widget directly in the email body, after the shipment

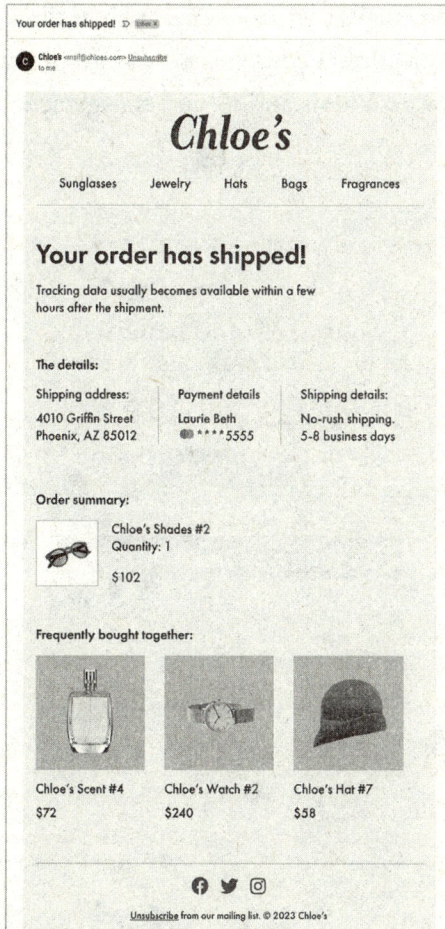

A fashion retailer's postpurchase emails include a recommendation widget leveraging the "purchased together" algorithm to highlight items commonly purchased alongside those already bought, encouraging additional spending

141

information. This will create a personalized, relevant experience for the customer that also anticipates future needs or desires based on their most recent purchase. Over time, this can increase retention and the number of average recurring orders per customer.

Activation Emails with Content Recommendations

Posttransaction emails can also include personalized recommendations for educational content, such as guides and blogs, to improve customer understanding and engagement.

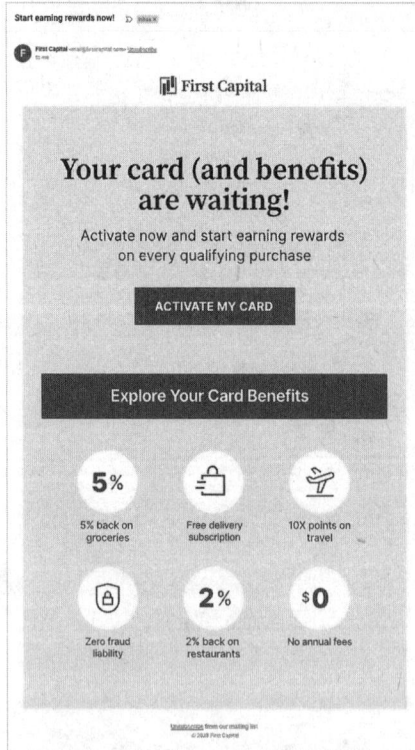

A leading bank uses a triggered email to encourage qualified customers to activate their new cobranded credit card, with content that educates on and incentivizes taking advantage of card benefits

TIME-BASED ABANDONMENT MESSAGES

The What: While cart abandonment is a natural occurrence, it shouldn't be seen as a lost cause. Brands can effectively recapture potentially lost sales through the strategic use of triggered emails. Sent automatically to a visitor based on their behavior—in this case, leaving a site with items in their cart—teams can use the opportunity as a reminder of what has been left behind, include personalized recommendations, and offer promotional deals to help close the conversion loop.

Time is of the essence: Cart abandonment emails sent within the first hour of abandonment perform best, so set up a campaign trigger to send an email instantly after the cart is abandoned.

The Why: Shopping cart and checkout abandonment are all too common behaviors among online shoppers. As our own data concludes, nearly three-fourths of site visitors abandon their carts—a stat that aggressively cuts into retail profits. As a result, many retailers have made abandonment reduction a primary goal and are devoting more resources toward achieving it. Fortunately, there are various tactics and personalization strategies that reduce cart abandonments to a minimum and induce greater ROI.

The How: If your customer has abandoned their cart, then there are a number of retargeting strategies and technologies you can leverage to encourage them to return. While online retargeting ads can be effective, marketers would be wise to invest in email campaigns that remain at the core of digital acquisition and customer retention. E-commerce brands can run personalized abandonment email campaigns to notify shoppers when out-of-stock items have been replenished or to offer discounts urging shoppers to complete the purchases they left behind.

Abandoned Cart Email Best Practices

There's no single right way to craft a killer abandoned cart email, but there are essentials and best practices you need to consider.

Get the Subject Line Down

The subject line is perhaps the most critical component of any email campaign. Continuously A/B test different catchy, personal, and straightforward subject lines to get a better sense of what works and what doesn't.

Crush the Copy

Stellar copy is the bread and butter of any remarketing email. While it can be tempting to get carried away in the process of creating a clever message, you must clearly address the following points in your copy:

- The shopper has left an item in their cart.
- The shopper was interested enough in the item to add it to their cart.
- The shopper needs to complete their order now.

Being unconventional can separate your email from the dozens of other promotional emails bombarding shoppers on a daily basis. Including an image of the actual product that was abandoned in the cart is a good idea, too.

Make It Clean, Keep It Pretty

Strikingly simple emails make the abandoned item the sole focus of a customer's attention. Include active links in the header that will take a customer back to different areas of the store—just in case they no longer want the item.

Additionally, shoppers tend to place a higher value on items that are in short supply. Pairing the scarcity principle with a sense of urgency can drastically improve your chances of recovering the sale.

Cross-Sell and Upsell

It may very well be that the shopper has already bought the abandoned item elsewhere. But this presents retailers with a tremendous opportunity to upsell and cross-sell. Retailers can achieve this by adding product recommendation units to the email, personalized according to the items that the shopper has demonstrated an interest in or items similar to what was abandoned in the cart.

Incentivize It

Unexpected costs and shipping fees are the overwhelming causes of cart abandonment. Many shoppers tend to calculate a final price by tallying the items without taking tax or shipping costs into account. Once the total is above expectation, it makes for an easy excuse to exit the site and continue shopping around.

Winning back customers who have been pushed away by a final price can be accomplished by highlighting your brand's unique value propositions (for example, free shipping and returns, warranties, elite customer service, and so on) or offering a discount.

There are a number of reasons shoppers abandon carts. It's upon you to invest the time to analyze your behavioral data to determine when, how, and for whom cart abandonment is occurring. Knowing how your shoppers behave will answer the question of whether or not you should be offering a discount.

See It in Action

Triggered Emails with Recommendations

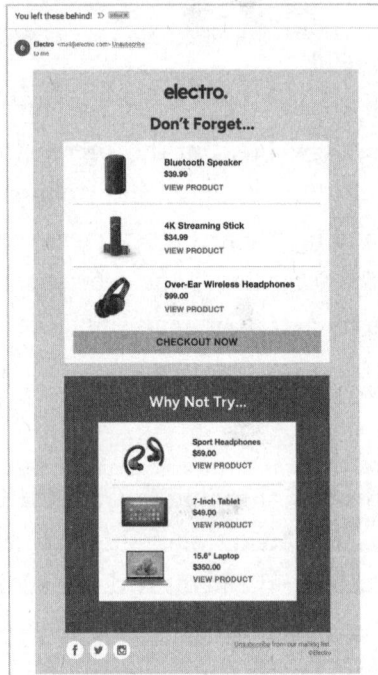

To recapture cart abandoners, a retailer targets visitors three hours after abandonment with triggered emails reminding them about items in their basket and inserting personalized recommendations

Real-Time Recommendation Widgets

Many of today's marketing emails are personalized at the time of send rather than when the email is opened, meaning the content and recommendations are predetermined and may not necessarily reflect the customer's most recent behavior, preferences, and intent. But with open-time email product recommendations, content can be presented when the recipient opens the email, resulting in every email being personalized for that specific moment in time, regardless of the time at which the email was sent.

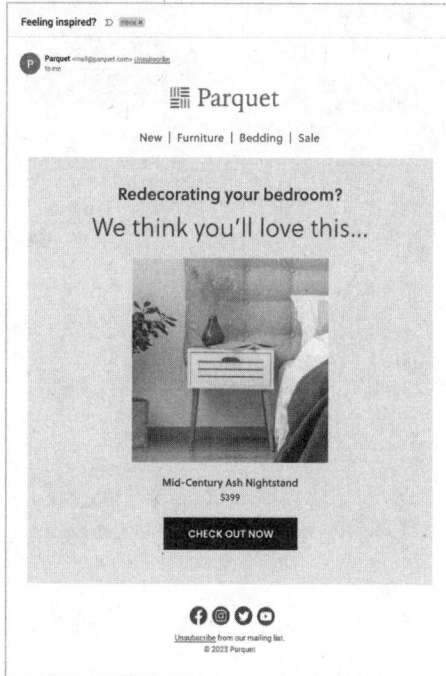

A furniture retailer embeds a widget in an email to recommend products related to recently viewed products in real time

Form or Application Reminders

Service-based businesses can also send triggered emails to abandoners, serving them reminders about unfinished forms or applications, then deep linking them back to the site, ensuring they can quickly pick up where they left off.

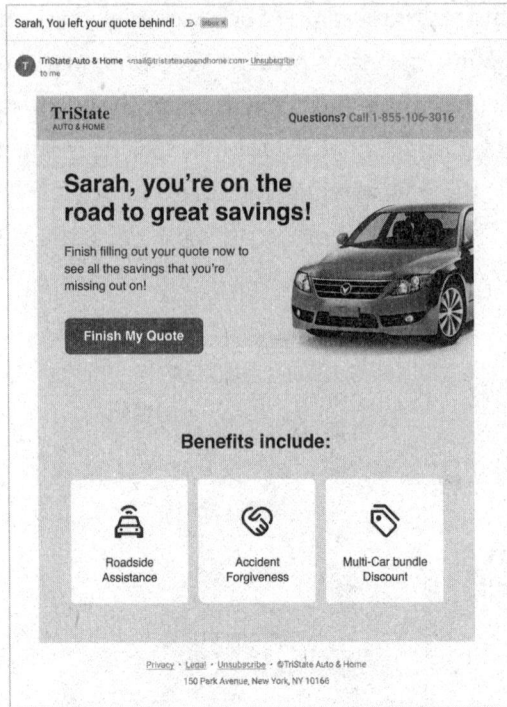

An insurance service company sends customers triggered emails based on their abandonment behavior, serving them reminders about unfinished quotes

EXIT-INTENT MESSAGES

The What: Exit-intent technology is an algorithm that detects and reacts to site abandonment in real time. Upon noticing exit intent (such as aggressive mouse movement to X-out of the page) the algorithm automatically triggers an incentivized pop-up to convince the abandoning visitor to take the desired action.

Exit pop-ups boil down your offering into a simple and concentrated version of whatever you're promoting. They narrow down the analysis required to make a decision. If done right, exit pop-ups can provide significant uplift and fulfill multiple revenue-based goals.

The Why: Sometimes visitors can be plagued by the paradox of choice, with too many options leading to analysis paralysis. In instances such as this, overwhelmed visitors may attempt to navigate away from the site. Before they do, brands can deploy exit-intent pop-ups to narrow down the decision-making process with elements such as recommendations personalized to the specific customer included in the messaging, compelling them to convert.

The How: Here are a few best practices for delivering exit-intent experiences.

Keep It Simple

Your exit pop-up should fulfill one goal. Only one goal. It should not be crammed with tons of content, multiple navigation mechanisms, or too many calls to action (CTAs). One goal: compel the customer to make a simple decision.

Putting too many CTAs or decisions in your pop-up is a recipe for confusion. Your message must make one point clearly and explicitly. If your goal is to capture newsletter sign-ups, don't also invite customers to "check out our new arrivals" or include another call to action that's unrelated to the goal at hand.

Additionally, any call to action on an exit pop-up should state exactly what will happen if the customer clicks on it. Instead of saying yes, no, cancel, or okay, on a call-to-action button, explicitly state your goal: "Yes, sign me up" or "Send me all the latest updates." Keep it simple: one pop-up, one clear decision.

A poorly designed exit pop-up spells disaster for decision-making and conversions. UI issues and bugs aside, some have so much content that they require a scroll bar or feature anchor links for other pages to send customers to.

Scrolling and anchor links make sense for lengthy web pages, not exit pop-ups.

Placing multiple navigation mechanisms or tons of text within a pop-up is an outdated approach that will distract the customer from the decision you're trying to convince them to make. A good rule to follow: If it's valuable info but needs a scroll, it should be its own page, not an exit pop-up.

Now, let's take a good look at how to use exit pop-ups to engage visitors who are keen on leaving your website.

Six Steps to Developing a Strong Exit Pop-Up Strategy

To produce the most effective exit pop-up campaigns, follow the SPROUT framework: Segment, Personalize, Recommend, Optimize, Urgency, Test.

1. Segment
You need to ask yourself the following two questions when creating a targeted offer using an exit pop-up: Who am I targeting? What action do I want them to take?

Who Am I Targeting?
The more targeted your pop-up is, the better your chances are of stopping site abandonment dead in its tracks. Instead of taking a one-size-fits-all approach, you can make your messaging segment- or context-specific. This entails making a conscious decision of what will work best for specific audience groups or pages rather than all your customers and your site in general.

- **Targeting by cohort:** Before you craft your copy, consider whom the offer is geared toward. Are you targeting first-time visitors? Cart abandoners? Price-sensitive shoppers? Paid traffic? Registered customers? Use your analytics data to get a good sense of your visitor's identity and then leverage audience segmentation accordingly. Taking the time to differentiate between behaviors, referral sources, and the intent of individual audience groups will help you deliver a far more powerful and relevant message.

- **Targeting by context:** Instead of taking a user-centric approach, you can take a context-centric one. Landing pages, home pages, blog pages, checkout pages, product pages, and category pages can all feature exit pop-ups unique to that page. If a customer is abandoning the home page, chances are they haven't interacted much with your brand or products. Triggering a welcome offer to home page abandoners, for example, can provide the necessary encouragement to engage further with your site.

It's important to note that contextual targeting isn't limited only to pages. Tailoring your message according to geolocation, device type, or local weather forecast is an especially effective method of creating relevant messages that resonate.

What Action Do I Want Them to Take?
Typically, exit pop-ups aim to get customers to view content, complete a form, or direct them to a specific or underlying page. Which desired action is the right one? It depends.

If your goal is for the customer to take in a short message (max two sentences), then having them either choose to convert on or dismiss the message makes sense. If your goal is to gain a subscription, then providing a bug-free form with one clear call-to-action is essential.

2. Personalize

A bona fide method of reigniting engagement is to layer personalization into your exit pop-ups according to each customer's interests and on-site behavior. You might consider tailoring and personalizing your message with dynamic variables such as:

- The customer's name
- Product affinities
- Real-time intent
- Subscription status

Making a personalized reference reinforces the emotional connection between the customer and your brand, demonstrates that your brand can identify their needs—both tactical and emotional—and can greatly increase your chances of reengagement.

3. Recommend

A very effective yet underused tactic is to use exit pop-ups to cross-sell and upsell products. Featuring personalized product recommendations in your exit pop-ups is a proven way to improve recirculation and reduce exit rates. Do this by first implementing automated recommendation widgets into the pop-up. Then, customize the widget's conditions to recommend according to the products the customer viewed or interacted with right before the abandonment.

4. Optimize

Pop-ups that feel easy and simple to customers are usually not the result of a quick and simple process. In order to create compelling exit pop-ups, you need to be constantly testing design, calls-to-action, and content. Continuous iteration and ongoing A/B testing and optimization are key to presenting the right message in the right context or to the right cohort.

A powerful approach to exit-intent optimization is to push multiple variations simultaneously and dynamically optimize the best-performing combinations according to specific objectives or KPIs. Exit pop-ups can be optimized according to goals— whether that goal is to improve click-through rate, generate more leads, or increase revenue, for instance, is up to you.

5. Create Urgency

Creating a sense of urgency is a great way to call visitors to action and encourage immediate decisions. Creating urgency with an exit pop-up means placing the customer in a situation where they will feel they are giving up on something valuable by choosing to navigate away.

You can create urgency by putting attention-grabbing keywords (for example, *% off*, *now*, *new*, *bestsellers*, *most popular*, and so on) within a given time frame (by midnight, today only, last call, only three hours left, and so on). Doing so will induce a fear of missing out and intrigue your shopper to seize the opportunity at hand rather than run from it.

6. Test

Organizations that deliver the most effective pop-ups are the ones that continuously iterate and analyze. Pay close attention to your data to see what's working and what isn't.

Just because a page can technically have an exit pop-up doesn't mean it should. Just because a message worked for one segment doesn't mean it will work for another. Just because an exit-intent tactic worked for your competitor doesn't mean it will work for you.

Exit-intent technology is an extremely effective way to induce conversions, leads, and recapture lost revenue. If done right, exit pop-ups will appeal to multiple customer segments in multiple contexts. No matter your objective, however, it's important to keep in mind that your goal is never to try and force the visitor to take an unwanted action. Exit pop-ups must entice the visitor to easily make one simple decision. The only way to deliver the most effective exit-intent messages is through constant analysis, testing, and using data to gain a better understanding of your customer base.

See It in Action

Personalized Recommendations

Personalizing recommendations is not only a guaranteed strategy for improving recirculation, increasing monetization, and reducing exit rates, but it is essential to providing shoppers guidance, encouraging them to complete their purchases and refrain from abandoning their carts. In a reality where most websites offer an overwhelming amount of content, customers may feel lost. Using sophisticated behavioral targeting algorithms, organizations can serve personalized and highly engaging messages to visitors upon display of exit intent.

Still looking for the right hotel? ×

Here is a selection of hotels you might like

★★★★☆
Epitome Resort & Spa
$510 AVG/NIGHT

BOOK NOW

★★★★★
Bronze Isle Resort
$700 AVG/NIGHT

BOOK NOW

★★★★★
Coastline Resort & Spa
$690 AVG/NIGHT

BOOK NOW

To boost bookings, this hotel reservation portal deploys microtargeted, personalized hotel and destination recommendations upon discovering exit intent to each of its visitors across the site

Personalized Offers

Let's say your visitor was just hit with unexpected shipping costs and has now decided to leave your site rather than proceeding

don't miss out on this great offer ending soon:

BUY 2, GET 1 FREE

FAVORITE SCIENCE FICTION

Recommended For You

Echoes of the Distant Sun
by Zaira Volin
★★★★★

Orbit of the Forgotten
by Nessa Varis
★★★★★

When Stars Fall Silent
by Kian Rhys
★★★★★

The Quantum Weaver
by Lyle Draymore
★★★★☆

To capture abandoning visitors, a bookseller deploys highly personalized exit-intent overlays featuring incentives for the categories and books visitors have affinities for alongside recommendations to checkout. Upon noticing your visitor's exit intent, you can effectively reengage them by automatically triggering an exit-intent overlay or notification with a targeted promotion for completing the order now.

Service and Assistance Messages

Brands with service-based solutions or more complex ordering processes can offer assistance options to solicit reengagement too.

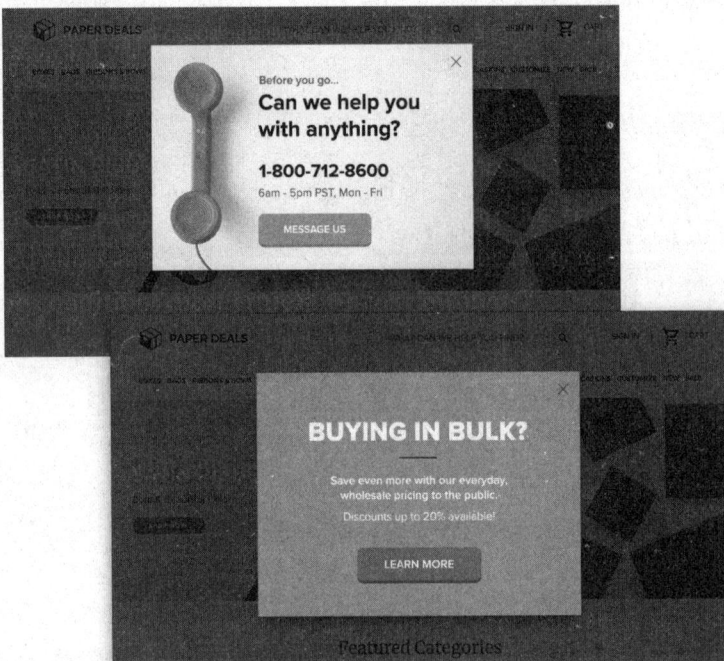

A wholesale retailer identifies customers based on account type and targets them with relevant pop-ups upon exit intent: B2B customers receive customer service messages (above) whereas promotions are surfaced for B2C customers (below)

A financial institution deploys triggered exit-intent overlays to prevent abandonment and drive application completions

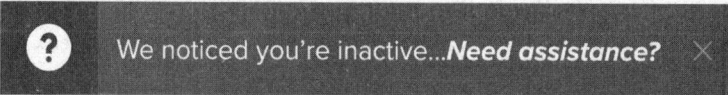

A bank programmed reminder notifications across pages, triggered to deploy when a customer is idle on the site, no matter their step in the conversion flow

Flashing Browser Tabs

It's typical behavior for online shoppers to toggle between several tabs per browsing session. But ensuring those visitors come back once they've navigated away from a site can be challenging because most tabs appear indistinguishable from one another and can get lost in the crowd. Flashing tabs can be used to drive consumers back to the shopping experience and toward a purchase.

● ● ●	**B** Shop Women's Fashion Onlin	×	New Tab	×
● ● ●	**B** We Miss You ♥	×	New Tab	×
● ● ●	**B** (1) You left item(s) in cart 🛒	×	New Tab	×

A fashion retailer deploys flashing tab notifications that change the title of the abandoned tab to grab the customer's attention if they already have items in their cart

PUSH NOTIFICATIONS AND SMS

The What: With its power to reach mobile users at critical moments, push notifications and SMS messages provide brands with the hook to retain customers, engaging them throughout the customer journey. All that's required is the right customer data to fuel and activate the right customized messages when it matters the most.

The Why: Today's consumers are constantly on their smartphones, making mobile a great channel for reengagement. But personalized notifications can be tricky, especially as consumers are being bombarded with ads and content from various organizations. With push notifications and SMS strategies, brands can capture a customer's attention in a captivating and optimally timed way. And by using customer behavior data, brands can ensure notifications are personalized and contextually relevant at any given moment.

The How: The marketing minds behind some of the most beloved apps out there have figured out how to leverage push marketing and SMS to their advantage. But many of these apps—like Netflix, Waze, and Uber—enjoy the advantage of a high-frequency customer base. What if you're in an industry with low engagement rates? Retail apps, in particular, are struggling to generate more app engagement using push notifications. Start by getting personal.

Market to People, Not Devices

People want personalized, relevant messages. They can easily sniff out generic, blasted messages that are part of an obvious reengagement campaign. Getting a meaningless message is an annoying distraction, and getting too many of them can lead the customer to stop buying from you altogether.

Personalization of push notifications and SMS, however, can deliver a considerable lift in open rates. One very effective and unconventional approach to personalizing these messages is to serve recommendations based on the products the customer has shown an affinity for in their browsing and buying history.

If a customer's behavior demonstrates that they are in the market for specific items—for example, they viewed and interacted with women's sneakers and workout apparel—then they could be served those items in the notification itself. What's more, deep linking to these products within your app enables customers to act on the notification instantly and drive increased conversions. Instead of opening the home screen, customers will find the notification to be increasingly relevant when it lands them directly on the product displayed.

Timeliness and Location-Based Push Notifications

If you're like most people, the last thing you want is to be woken up by your phone buzzing at 2:00 a.m. by a message from an e-commerce app. Stories of badly timed notifications abound for two reasons:

- The times marketers send notifications and times customers are actually opening and engaging with them are out of sync, often resulting in out-of-date messaging.
- Marketers often totally miss time zones—for example, in Europe, the Middle East, and Africa, marketers send messages at midnight, when most customers are sleeping—as they focus on hitting peak times in North America instead of creating local campaigns.

The solution to the timeliness problem is to customize delivery time according to demonstrated behavior or send the notification at the time each customer is most likely to engage based on the actions they have already taken.

When Is the Right Time to Send the Message?

You can start by creating conditions to send the message based on the customer's most active or last active period. For example, if a customer has a history of engaging at 6:00 p.m. and purchasing around 8:00 p.m., then marketers can create conditions to send the message at 8:00 p.m. when the customer is most likely to purchase.

The solution to the location problem is to geotarget customers and send messages according to each customer's local time zone.

Marketers can even tailor specific promotional messages based on the customer's local weather conditions.

It's also important to point out that location-based notifications do not have to be limited to online shopping: Retailers with brick-and-mortar stores can encourage physical store visits by triggering an incentivizing message to customers that are nearby.

Recover Abandoned Shopping Carts

Combating shopping cart abandonment is a major challenge for all online retailers, and this is especially true with mobile.

Shoppers abandon their carts for a number of reasons (be it high shipping costs, more affordable alternatives, window shopping, and so on), and while sending cart abandonment emails is an invaluable tactic to recover sales from abandoned carts, open rates for push notifications are 50 percent higher than for email, and click rates are up to twice as high.

You can proactively increase mobile conversions by pushing messages to a segment of customers who abandoned your mobile website or app after beginning checkout.

Most apps don't have a cart abandonment strategy in place and have no way to nudge customers to complete their purchases. Reminding customers that they have unpurchased items in their carts is a critical tactic to win back those lost purchase opportunities.

Push notifications and SMS messages are one of the most effective ways for marketers to incentivize mobile reengagement and drive retention. Perfectly timed and personalized messages delight customers, while irrelevant and spammy push messages and SMS will drive them away.

It's critical to keep in mind that push notifications and SMS—like all one-to-one messages—represent ongoing interactions with your customers that must be tested and optimized. Make sure to monitor your customer data over time to understand the effect each notification has on different customer segments and the role mobile messaging plays in your overall marketing strategy.

See It in Action

Automatic Reminders

Send a text-based message to a customer when they haven't opened your mobile app in over a week, forgot to finish filling out a form, or more.

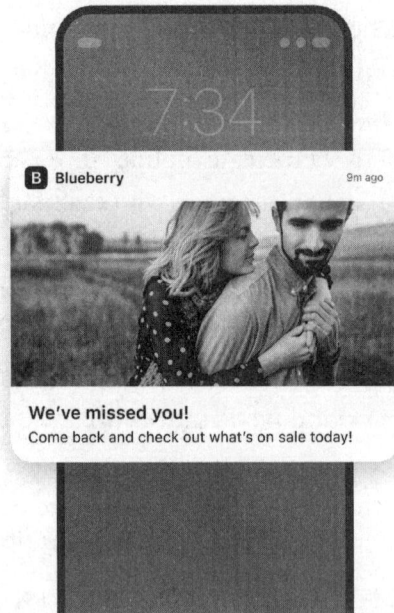

A retailer urged customers back to its app with an optimized push notification that includes rich content and a personalized image

A retailer proactively increased mobile conversions by pushing notifications to a segment of customers who abandoned its mobile website or app after beginning checkout

Recover Abandoned Carts

If a customer leaves items in their shopping cart without checking out, send them a push notification or SMS including the products left behind to recover a potentially lost purchase.

A retailer ensures returning customers to its app store with this rich push notification experience that includes a personalized product recommendations slider

Deliver Product Recommendations

Send VIP customers a message highlighting recommended products they might be interested in if a purchase hasn't been completed in the last two weeks.

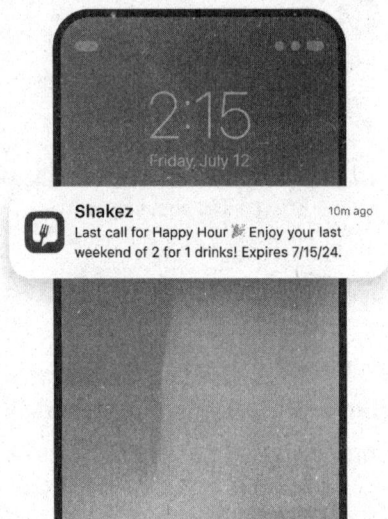

A restaurant used a push notification to bring a two-for-one drink deal top of mind, driving customers back to the app and increasing both engagement and revenue overall

Send Custom Offers

Create and send a personalized push notification featuring limited offers and expiration deadlines using the triggers and targeting conditions most critical for your business.

CONTINUOUS ENGAGEMENT AND OPTIMIZATION

✖ ✤ ✖ ✳

This category highlights use cases that focus on keeping customers engaged and informed while also gathering valuable feedback to continuously improve the customer experience. By understanding customer behavior and preferences, these use cases help optimize the experience for better engagement and conversions over time.

- **Social Proof and Product Demand Messaging:** Leverages the actions or opinions of others to engage customers, making the experience feel livelier and more connected.
- **Promotional Messaging:** Engages customers with marketing messages that are specifically tailored to their behaviors and preferences, encouraging more meaningful engagement.
- **Time-Sensitive Messaging and Offers:** Encourages immediate action by delivering messages or offers that capitalize on the moment's urgency or specific timing.
- **Customer Journey Continuity:** Aims to create a seamless and coherent experience across various

interactions, ensuring consistency throughout the customer journey.

SOCIAL PROOF AND PRODUCT DEMAND MESSAGING

The What: While we'd like to think our actions are always determined by our own individualistic thinking, the truth is that our final decision-making is often conditioned by those around us. Social proof is a psychological phenomenon where people assume the actions of others in an attempt to reflect correct behavior for a given situation. In essence, it's the notion that since others are doing it, you should be doing it too. Social proof is especially prominent in situations where people are unable to determine the appropriate mode of behavior and is driven by the assumption that surrounding people possess more knowledge about the situation.

The Why: Social proof is especially salient in the realm of online shopping, and brands can use it to subtly push hesitant visitors to purchase.

Even if a brand's unique value proposition is perfect, it may not be enough to secure a purchase. Studies have shown that peer reviews can be twelve times more influential on customers than a merchant's description.

Leveraging social proof in your offering can solidify customer confidence in purchasing decisions and help eliminate the concerns that stand between them and clicking the buy button.

The How: The following are best practices for creating social proof campaigns across channels.

Highlight High Customer Demand

Highlighting demand for a product is a proven method of boosting sales and can be accomplished by showcasing the number of views, adds to cart, or purchases that were conducted within a specific time frame. Notifying customers that "157 people have bought this product within the last twenty-four hours," for example, creates a correlation between urgency and buying in the customer's mind and induces a fear of missing out for not going through with the purchase.

The understanding that other people have already bought the item plays an important role in validating the customer's own thinking to buy it as well. Uncertain customers naturally find comfort in a greater collective, and if you can create the impression that everyone is buying your product, there's a strong likelihood that they will too.

The Principle of Community

Human beings have a tendency to turn to others when determining courses of action, especially those who come from similar backgrounds or share similar interests. Brands can leverage this idea by evoking a sense of identity when presenting products to customers.

One way to accomplish this is by inserting a product badge or overlay that makes direct reference to a customer's geolocation. If a customer is from New York, for instance, communicating that an additional "98 visitors are now viewing this item in New York" lends credibility to the product and creates a relatable outlet for the customer. Allowing customers to "feel at home" when buying is a bona fide way of increasing purchase rates.

Building trust is key to reducing friction and reassuring customers. Surfacing positive customer testimonials in the right context can achieve exactly that.

Don't Forget to Test!

Leveraging social proof marketing remains one of the most effective ways to ease the minds of apprehensive customers and successfully influence purchasing decisions.

When it comes to introducing social proofing tactics into your marketing, be sure to A/B test your ideas as you implement them to find the variations that make the most sense for your audience segments. Ongoing optimization can make all the difference when persuading visitors using the power of social proof.

See It in Action

Highlight Testimonials or Trust Badges

Purchasing from a new brand or company can feel unfamiliar and often requires a bit more emotional labor when it comes to making a purchase decision. Brands can empathize with these feelings and establish a layer of trust.

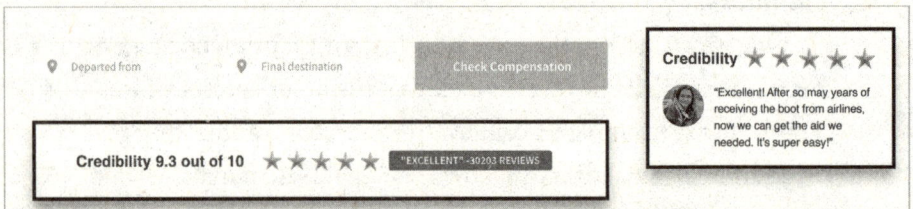

Departed from	Final destination	Check Compensation	Credibility ★ ★ ★ ★ ★

Credibility 9.3 out of 10 ★ ★ ★ ★ ★ "EXCELLENT" -30203 REVIEWS

"Excellent! After so may years of receiving the boot from airlines, now we can get the aid we needed. It's super easy!"

An airline passenger protection company uses social proof to highlight testimonials and trust badges in a prominent home page location to boost decision-making confidence and increase bookings

Show Demand Messaging

If brands can create the impression that everyone is buying a product, there's a strong likelihood that new customers will too. One way to accomplish this is by inserting a notification that directly references how many times the product has been viewed or purchased in the last week, incentivizing shoppers to complete their purchase and increasing purchase rates.

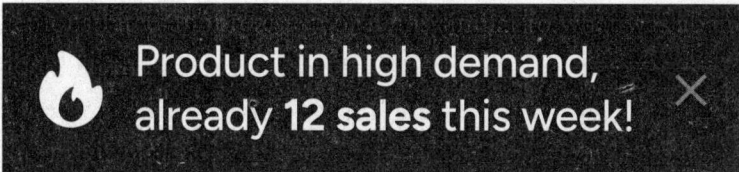

Product in high demand, already **12 sales** this week!

A retailer displays demand messaging via notifications on its PDPs to drive customers to make a purchase alongside the other X number of those who purchased in the same week

PROMOTIONAL MESSAGING

The What: Promotional messaging stands as a key strategy for engaging customers and driving sales. This approach involves crafting offers and messages that are genuinely aligned with the individual's preferences, behaviors, and purchase history. The power of promotional messaging lies in its ability to deliver targeted discounts, exclusive deals, and personalized recommendations that not only grab the customer's attention but also significantly increase the likelihood of conversion.

The Why: The digital marketplace is inundated with brands vying for consumer attention, making it increasingly challenging to stand out. In this context, generic marketing messages often fall flat, failing to engage the modern consumer who expects personalized experiences. Promotional messaging addresses this challenge head-on by leveraging data analytics and customer insights to tailor communications that resonate on a personal level. This targeted approach not only enhances the customer experience but also fosters a sense of value and recognition, leading to deeper brand loyalty.

By focusing on individual preferences and behaviors, promotional messaging enables businesses to create more meaningful connections with their audience. These connections drive engagement and retention because customers are more likely to interact with and purchase from brands that recognize their unique needs and interests.

The How: To implement an effective promotional messaging strategy, businesses must navigate the delicate balance between offering value and maintaining profitability. For example:

Limited-Time Offers

Introduce time-sensitive discounts or offers to create a sense of urgency. These can act as powerful incentives for customers to reengage with your brand, particularly if they perceive the offer as exclusive or valuable.

Segmented Offers

Segment your audience based on their activity levels, preferences, and purchasing history. This allows for the delivery of personalized promotions at scale. Automation can also help manage the frequency of messages, ensuring customers are not overwhelmed by too many offers.

See It in Action

Targeted Promotions by Customer Journey Status

Different pages and stages in the customer journey require different promotional strategies. For example, serving a visitor a coupon for 10 percent off makeup accessories while they are browsing for hair care products likely wouldn't elicit a sale. But a brand can match promotional messaging according to page type, the customer's activity, past purchase behavior, and other factors. The more relevant the experience, the greater the chance the shopper will take you up on the offer.

10% OFF YOUR FIRST ORDER	FREE RETURNS	FREE GIFT WITH PURCHASE
Enter WELCOME10 at checkout	Find out more	On select items

A beauty brand shows a site-wide "skinny-banner" with three offers most relevant based on the specific page type, performance, and the customer's progress in the conversion funnel

Exit-Intent Offers

Consumers aren't strangers to research. With endless options available at their fingertips, customers tend to shop around to find the best deal possible. With such stiff competition, deploying smart merchandising strategies can not only grab a customer's attention but also prevent them from abandoning your site. Consider waiting to offer coupons or discounts until a customer shows signs of abandonment, noted by cursor movement or highlighting a product name.

SURPRISE!

A coupon is available for this item. Get **20% off** at checkout with our code.

USE CODE **ENTER20**

A brand loads a surprise coupon code for visitors who are highlighting the product name with the intention of price-shopping in another tab, reducing abandonment and eliciting conversions

Get 15% off with your personal code: **BM1DX!** Expiring on 24/10/2024

A hotel network improves booking rates by serving visitors with personalized, time-sensitive coupons based on their likelihood to book a room currently in view

Bottom Bar Notifications by Audience Segment

One way to encourage site visitors to engage with bottom bar notifications is by prioritizing different messages for different audience segments, ensuring each call to action resonates with whom it is being served to. For example, encourage cart abandoners or customers who have browsed multiple products to complete a purchase by offering "free two-day shipping" using the bottom bar notification.

🎁 **Bundle & Save!**		📏 **Find your perfect fit.**	
Get $40 off & Free Shipping	✕	**Take our fit finder quiz.**	✕
Shop Now →		Get Started →	

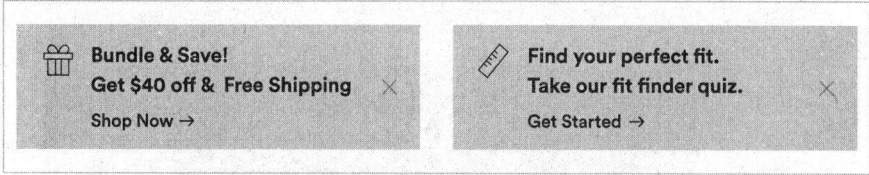

A retailer created and served contextualized bottom bar banner notifications according to different audiences' site behavior on both mobile and desktop to keep them engaged at every stage

Triggered Emails with Offers

Promotional messaging isn't limited to on-site activations, either. To increase activation on promotions, you can target specific coupons to the audiences most likely to act on your email offers.

Thank you for your recent purchase
Here's a **20% off** coupon for your next order   `20NDOFF`

A retailer sent emails with a 20 percent off coupon only to customers who purchased in the past thirty days, increasing email conversion rate and overall purchases

Price Drop Emails

Customers may not be ready to buy unless the price is right, and you want to ensure that money is, in fact, the reason why a shopper didn't go through with a purchase. Set up with a minimum threshold in mind and capped at a particular frequency, a price drop email campaign can recover lost sales while being mindful of profit margins.

New price alert!

Wide Convertible Sofa
~~$481.00~~ **$325.99**

CHECKOUT NOW

A retailer automatically triggers an email for shoppers who engaged with a product but did not buy, notifying them that it has been reduced in price to encourage purchase completion

Demand Messaging

Additionally, the use of time-sensitive messages is powerful to get customers to act fast and act now. The fear of missing out is real—shoppers are motivated to purchase when confronted with the knowledge that an item is available or on sale only for a limited time, low in stock, or in high demand. Brands can capitalize on this by incorporating demand messaging into their strategy, highlighting important information to keep visitors in the loop. This can take shape in the form of product badges, notifications, push notifications, messaging, and more. In a reality where presenting a perfect value proposition isn't always enough, grasping the psychology behind consumer decisions is key to driving sales and increasing conversions.

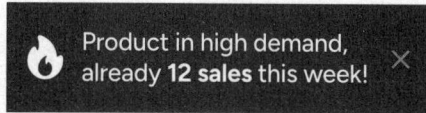

> 🔥 Product in high demand,
> already **12 sales** this week! ✕

To push visitors toward checkout, a fashion group serves customers a notification when viewing a product that is on sale for a limited time, urging them to complete their purchase before missing out

Countdown Timers

Additionally, including a countdown can help increase urgency and move the customer to act, decreasing and preventing attrition of at-risk customers.

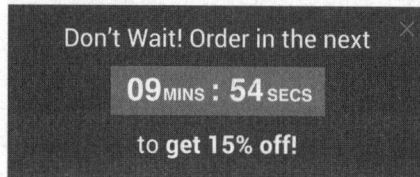

> Don't Wait! Order in the next ✕
>
> **09**MINS **:** **54**SECS
>
> to **get 15% off!**

A retailer drives visitors to purchase by introducing an exclusive, time-sensitive promotion that, once accepted, initiates a countdown displaying how long it will remain in effect

> ✕
>
> **Countdown to cash back!**
>
> Spend $1000 on your card before September 1st to unlock a $150 cash bonus
>
> Offer ends in:
>
> | Days | Hours | Minutes | Seconds |
> | **01** : **07** : **44** : **34** |

A fintech company leverages predictive spend data to identify and target customers likely to disengage from their cards, delivering personalized time-bound offers on mobile web and app

175

Countdown to College

Open a student account by September 1st and earn a one-time **$150 cash bonus.**

Offer ends in...

02 **01** **21** **56**
DAYS HRS MIN SEC

APPLY NOW

7867 5678 2364 5978

M HARRY CALLAHAN

A bank launched an overlay message, using countdown timers with urgency tactics to promote time-sensitive offers and campaigns

Exit-Intent Offers

Sometimes shoppers will get all the way to the cart page after browsing and carefully making their selections only to question whether or not the purchase is worth it in the end. In cases like this, retailers can deploy time-sensitive promotions, high-lighted during the checkout process, to validate the shopper's decision to move forward and buy. This can be personalized for different audience segments based on factors like the value of items in-cart or the individual's likelihood of engaging with the promotion.

FREE SHIPPING SITEWIDE & FREE $20 GIFT CARD! | OFFER ENDS IN: **09**hrs **57**min **59**sec

A retailer personalizes a top banner with time-sensitive promotions for different audiences, which are automatically added to the visitor's cart during checkout

CUSTOMER JOURNEY CONTINUITY

The What: Today's consumers typically interact with a company across channels, perhaps browsing a site once, then clicking on an email, and later scrolling through a mobile app. These interactions should feel cohesive. There is much that can be done pre- and postclick to optimize the customer experience, and the best way to do that is to acknowledge what brought them to your site in the first place. Continuity is key during these initial, critical moments in the relationship, and failing to take context into consideration when interacting with a prospective customer for the first time may send them away disillusioned, driving them to find what they were looking for somewhere else.

The Why: In today's world, consumers are surrounded by technology. On average, each person has more than six connected devices, ranging from smartphones and laptops to smart TVs and gaming consoles. This interconnectedness has fundamentally changed consumer expectations. While customers seamlessly switch between these devices throughout the day, they expect a consistent customer experience across all of them.

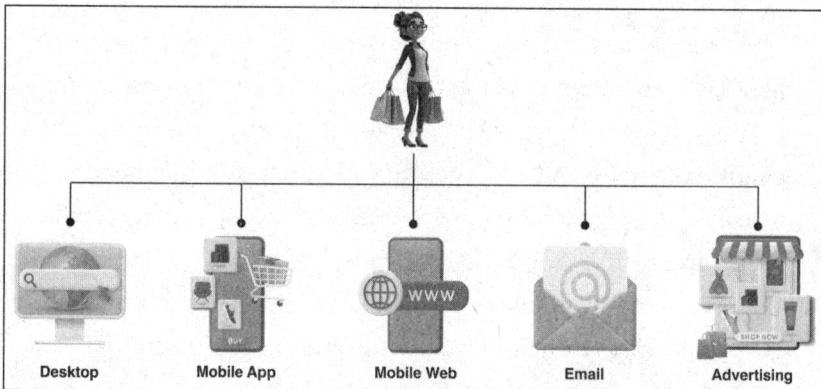

| Desktop | Mobile App | Mobile Web | Email | Advertising |

This is the idea behind "omnichannel," and it means that businesses need to ensure their brand presence and interactions are consistent, regardless of the device a customer is using. Whether it's browsing a website on a desktop computer or making a purchase through a mobile app, the experience should be smooth, intuitive, and meet the customer's needs.

The How: These best practices will help you create a continuous customer journey across channels:

Match Landing Page Messaging with Ad Copy

Akin to a customer receiving a print offer to redeem at a brick-and-mortar location only to be met by representatives lacking information or context, serving ad copy inconsistent with the landing page experience is one of the quickest ways to deter conversions. Marketers need to ensure continuity when an individual arrives at a site from an affiliate link or is referred via a certain marketing campaign.

Change the Landing Page Experience for Different Segments

The more a landing page connects with customers, the more likely it is to convert. Marketers, therefore, need to reconsider how often generic experiences make their way into new campaigns. Catchall landing pages may be easier to implement but usually end up generating lower-yielding results, wasting media spend and time.

Instead, all available data should be leveraged to establish buyer personas, from which unique landing pages can then be created, served, and optimized per audience.

Beyond basic demographics, the consumers' location, weather, device type, affinities, and more can all be used to segment new and anonymous customers. Once known, more behavioral insights, such as browsing history and interest displayed in certain products or services, can be layered in.

Bring the Customer Back to Context

Today's customers commit to doing research before shopping and many don't make a decision to purchase on their first visit—especially in luxury and higher-risk categories like banking and insurance. Marketers in these cases should expect a high degree of site abandonment during the initial steps of the decision process. With articles, recommendations, reviews, and terms to weigh, prospects will be in a haze of information, which provides you the perfect opportunity to offer relief.

Using data collected from previous interactions and browsing history, prospects can be brought back into context via triggered emails or personalized messages directing them to pick up where they left off—a service in and of itself. Remembering the key benefits associated with a particular product or promotion, consumers will be one step closer to sealing the deal.

See It in Action

Let Customers Pick Up Where They Left Off

Site visitors are busy and on the go, and sometimes it can be difficult for customers to finish a task they have started while engaging with your site. Displaying a welcome message upon reentry that guides customers back to where they left off caters to a site visitor's individual journey, allowing them to quickly complete any unfinished task.

A financial services company increases form completions through web notifications when customers who started completing an application return to the site

E-commerce brands can resurface previously viewed products to create a similarly positive experience for shoppers.

A beauty brand identifies returning customers and surfaces the product and category that they have previously browsed in an overlay

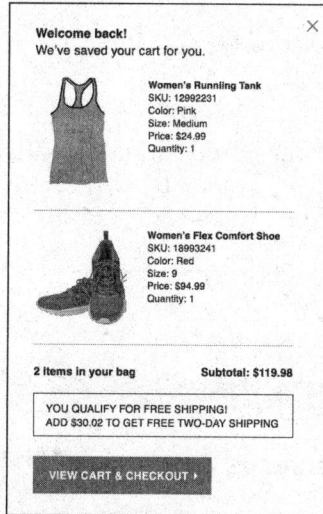

A fashion retailer saves abandoners' carts for them when they return to the site, greeting them with a welcome message and note that they've saved their cart along with a "Checkout" button

This strategy can be replicated on mobile web and mobile apps too.

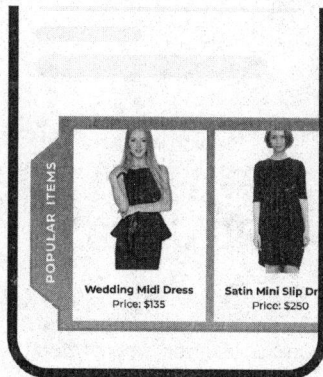

Ideal for the limited real estate available on mobile screens, this recommendation drawer offers an unintrusive and super-handy discovery solution when people are browsing endless products. It eliminates losing track of what has been viewed on your smartphone

Create Message Continuity

The best way to welcome a newly acquired customer is by acknowledging the value proposition that attracted them in the first place.

A financial services company creates landing pages for each respective ad it launches (connected via URL parameters) to ensure customers are directed to the call to action that originally piqued their interest

A finance company personalizes welcome notifications for each customer according to their affiliate traffic source, creating a consistent experience between the two sites

A retailer displays notifications to new customers, acknowledging the podcast or referring domain that sent the customer to their shop

Integration with Your Marketing Stack

Brands can create an omnichannel customer journey experience by integrating their data solutions and platforms with a personalization engine and sharing data across marketing stacks.

A financial organization surfaces personalized offers and content across the site, app, and email based on each customer's brand affinity, spending power, and preferences

Omnichannel personalization isn't limited to just digital channels either. You can connect your person-to-person experiences, like call-center data too.

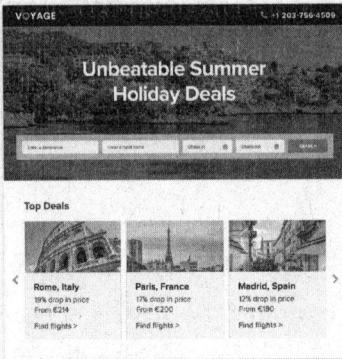

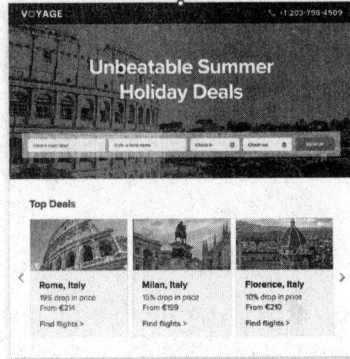

A travel booking company connects online and offline experiences by targeting high-value leads that have contacted its call center, using data from the call to personalize offers and messaging while they are still active online: The default home page (left) is personalized on the next visit after a user calls to ask about vacations in Italy but doesn't complete the booking (right)

THE FUTURE OF PERSONALIZATION

A successful personalization program combines the right technology, expertise, processes, methodologies, and strategies to meet the new standard of customer expectations and to pave the way for exceeding them. The organizations that invest in their personalization programs and get this right will be seen as pioneers, redefining how customers create a lasting emotional connection with brands and navigate the digital world.

But where does human ingenuity fit into the future AI-driven marketing era?

Machines have proven to be indispensable when it comes to scaling frequent, high-volume tasks, but they fall short when confronted with unique and unexpected situations where human creativity, adaptability, and ingenuity are needed. Simply put, machines cannot empathize with humans.

Machines excel at the predictable. They churn out repetitive tasks with unerring accuracy, tirelessly analyzing data and optimizing processes.

Humans, on the other hand, prevail through chaos and uncertainty. During the Apollo 13 mission, an oxygen tank explosion damaged the spacecraft, creating a life-threatening situation.

Despite limited resources and unpredictable conditions, the astronauts and ground control engineers improvised solutions using onboard materials and innovative thinking. Their ability to adapt to an unprecedented crisis ultimately saved the astronauts' lives, showcasing the power of human ingenuity in the face of chaos.

This story (and many others) highlights our uniquely human ability to improvise, adapt, and draw connections where none were previously seen. Our unpredictable brains thrive on novelty, finding inspiration in the seemingly random and crafting solutions from the unexpected. This is where our true advantage lies.

As a marketer, think about creating captivating copy that cuts through the noise or designing a unique customer experience that changes consumer behavior—these are not products of careful predictions and algorithmic calculations but of human intuition, empathy, and creativity.

By establishing the right center of excellence for your personalization program, you'll set up your organization to make the most of both opportunities. Think of it as a grand symphony: Machines keep the tempo while the humans feel, observe, and connect, creating the memorable melody that drives the art form forward. Their power lies in the efficient and the predictable, while ours resides in the imaginative and the adaptable.

To thrive in this era, we must embrace our distinctly human strengths.

Nurture Creativity

Engage in activities that spark imagination and divergent thinking. Divergent thinking helps break free from predictable patterns and deliver truly personalized experiences. By tapping into our unique human strengths, we can create experiences that are not only relevant but also emotionally resonant, unexpected, and truly delightful.

Cultivate Empathy

Seek out diverse perspectives and be empathetic to your customers' unique pain points, needs, and desires. In today's hyperconnected world, differentiation is truly about understanding your customers on a human level and weaving that understanding into every thread of your brand experience. That's where empathy comes in. This understanding of your customer landscape empowers you to craft experiences that resonate on a deeper level, addressing not just the functional problems customers face but the emotional desires that fuel their actions.

Balance Relevance and Respect

Focus on building trust with customers, emphasize the responsible design and handling of personalized experiences, and highlight autonomy over data. Personalization should be done in a way that respects the privacy of the individual. This will ensure that the brand's efforts do not come off as creepy to the customer but, instead, reflect their needs and interests in a way that is natural to their relationship with the brand.

The future belongs to those who not only harness the power of artificial intelligence marketing but also amplify human ingenuity's boundless potential.

TRANSMISSION FROM YOUR PERSONALIZED FUTURE:

THE SIGNAL NEVER FADES

You've reached the end of these transmissions after exploring the foundations, delving into the business of creating them, and building your own personalization playbook brimming with strategies for critical customer experience themes.

Remember: Your future is not a fixed destination. Like personalization, it's a constantly evolving landscape, shaped by your choices and actions. This book has equipped you with the tools to navigate it and translate the faint signals into clear pathways.

Don't stop tuning in. Keep experimenting, learning, and most importantly, bringing the human connection to the forefront. By fostering genuine interaction and tailoring experiences, you'll build a strong business funnel and even stronger relationships with your customers.

We hope this book serves as a valuable resource on your journey. The future beckons, waiting for you to write your own transmission. Go forth and personalize it.

ACKNOWLEDGMENTS

We are grateful to the many people at Dynamic Yield over the years who have played pivotal roles in shaping the perspectives, best practices, and methodologies within this book. In a world increasingly shaped by AI, their expertise, insights, and creativity offer a powerful testament to the enduring value human ingenuity and empathy bring to the table.

We offer special appreciation to Dynamic Yield's leadership team, notably Ori Bauer (chief executive officer), Einat Haftel (chief product officer), and Gidi Vigo (vice president of product), whose guidance and support have been instrumental throughout this endeavor.

Additionally, we wish to acknowledge the following individuals for their invaluable contributions: Ben Malki, Doron Taub, Elizabeth Shew, Erika Whitestone, Ernie Santeralli, Gemma Green, Marcel Rduch, Sam Macleod, Vivian Ly, and Yonatan Ido.

INDEX

Page numbers followed by *f* and *t* refer to figures and tables, respectively.

ABOUT THE AUTHORS

LIZ STEELMAN is a storyteller and content strategist specializing in brand marketing. She has shaped the editorial voice for high-growth technology companies like InVision and Wix, and began her career as a writer and editor at Time Inc. and Apartment Therapy Media. Liz is passionate about crafting compelling narratives that connect brands with their audiences and drive meaningful engagement.

SHANA PILEWSKI is a recognized authority in personalization, dedicated to advancing thought leadership and fostering knowledge-sharing across the industry. She frequently contributes as a subject matter expert, educating the market on how to turn personalization into a competitive business differentiator while shaping best practices and driving its adoption as a critical driver of success.

YANIV NAVOT is a marketing leader and personalization expert with nearly two decades of experience driving performance-driven marketing at scale. As chief marketing officer at Dynamic Yield, he shaped the personalization market and led the company's rise as an industry leader. Joining as the first marketing hire, Yaniv built a world-class team and partnered with top B2C brands to deliver impactful, cutting-edge personalization strategies.